SELF-DECORATION IN MOUNT HAGEN

ART AND SOCIETY SERIES
Edited by Peter J. Ucko

SELF-DECORATION IN MOUNT HAGEN

Andrew and Marilyn Strathern

GERALD DUCKWORTH & CO LTD
3, HENRIETTA STREET, LONDON W.C.2

First published in 1971 by
Gerald Duckworth & Company Limited,
3, Henrietta Street, London W.C.2.

© *Andrew and Marilyn Strathern 1971*

ISBN 0 7156 0516 X

Printed in Great Britain
by Jarrold & Sons Ltd, Norwich

CONTENTS

LIST OF PLATES

LIST OF COLOUR PLATES *(between pages 164 and 165)*

LIST OF FIGURES

LIST OF TABLES

NOTE ON ORTHOGRAPHY

We use three special symbols in the transcription of Melpa words.

1. ø   this is a tense, rounded, half-close, front-central vowel, pronounced as is 'u' in 'murder' (southern English pronunciation).

    Example: køi ('bird')

2. rl   this combination of letters represents a partially retroflexed and palatalised lateral 'l', pronounced similarly to 'rl' in 'world' (American English pronunciation).

    Example: mørli ('girl's dance')

3. raised ^{e} this is a lax, unrounded, mid-central vowel, the schwa, pronounced as is the final 'a' in 'banana'.

    Example: wu^e ('man')

To our parents

'Faith, there's a dozen of 'em, with delicate fine
hats and most courteous feathers, which bow the head
and nod at every man.'

All's Well that Ends Well, IV, 5

'Farewell the plumed troop and the big wars
That make ambition virtue!'

Othello, III, 3

PREFACE

'Primitive art' usually brings to mind certain kinds of art objects: statues, paintings, masks and so on. Some of the New Guinea societies – for example, those in the Sepik area – are famous for their art of this type, but the Hageners, who form the subjects of this book, do little carving, painting, or mask-making (see Appendix II). Instead, they concentrate on self-decoration. Often in other parts of New Guinea art objects are representations of ancestors or spirits, constructed for cult performances, and they convey messages about values held by the society in which they are made. In Hagen many of these messages are communicated by the decorations which performers at cults and exchange-festivals themselves wear.[1]

All over New Guinea people ornament themselves for important occasions, and in this Hageners are like other New Guineans. Such self-decoration is something more than a matter of fashion and cosmetics. In Hagen it is a medium through which people demonstrate their relationship to their ancestral spirits, express certain ideals and emotions, in short make statements about social and religious values.

In his book on Primitive Art, Adam[2] remarked that in New Guinea almost all implements, whether they have a ritual or technical use, receive some kind of decoration. In Hagen, however, only items connected with cults, exchange-festivals, or warfare are ornamented with any elaboration.[3] Such items also tend to be decorated in the same way as are people themselves and to be carried or worn by people. In one sense they are part of the whole process of self-decoration. In another sense their decoration is secondary to the primary emphasis which Hageners place on adorning their own bodies.

Thus we are dealing with art objects of a kind, but the objects are human beings.

I

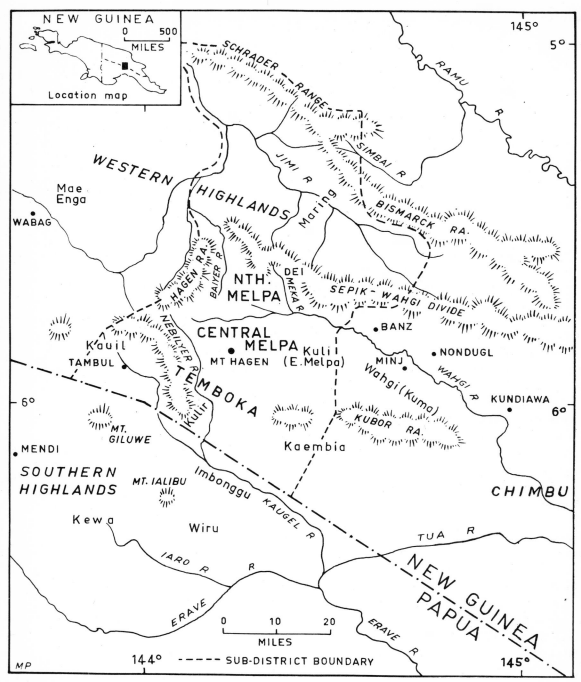

The Hagen sub-district

CHAPTER ONE

The setting

INTRODUCTION

Hagen is a competitive society. Within it there are no hereditary offices of chief-ship nor any rigid hierarchical relations. Its small political groups and their self-made leaders (called 'big-men') are continually competing for temporary advantages over each other. The main arena for this competition is an elaborate ceremonial exchange system (the *moka*), in which groups try to outdo each other by the size of their gifts of shell valuables and pigs. In this exchange system there is a strong contrast between the status and activities of the men and those of the women. Men controlled warfare in the past (which the Australian Administration stopped in 1945), and formally control exchange transactions today; women raise children and pigs, tend gardens, and link clans together by their marriages, although the marriages are most often arranged by men.

Hagen decorations reflect these factors. They are most frequently worn for temporary displays at dances held to celebrate achievements in the exchange system. Decorations do not mark out lasting relations of superiority and inferiority, but are assertions that one's own group has succeeded in a current bout of exchanges. Such political occasions are largely dominated by men, and men also control cult performances. It is consistent with this situation that, although women do decorate themselves for special occasions, they do not take a prominent part in the formal displays at festivals and cults so frequently as men.

Nevertheless, for men and women alike, festivals for which the most elaborate

Plate 1
Dancers march through
a throng of spectators

decorations are made are occasions to be looked forward to. Plans and preparations involve not only the main participants, their wives and families, but
also a wide network of kin and friends who are called on for help. When
festivals are staged they also attract visitors from surrounding areas. One mark
of an occasion's success, in fact, is the size of the crowd that is drawn to watch
the display (Pl. 1).

Exchange festivals proceed in regular sequences between neighbouring groups
in an area. For example, several minor exchanges may take place between the
segments of a large group, followed by a major festival, in which all the segments
take part in giving to outside recipients. In a year when a group is building up
resources towards a major festival, some of its members are involved almost
continually in dancing and in exchange transactions. Another year, their
participation may be limited to appearances as visitors at other people's festivals.

Decorations and dances are always designed for effect: the aim is to impress
spectators and the other dancers. The participants have to make sure not only
that the actual gifts they make are adequate, but that their bodily appearance is

Plate 2
Displays take place at
ceremonial grounds
specially planted with
trees and shrubs

fitting also. Weeks of practice dancing may precede a final display, and on
each new day of dancing a whole assemblage of ornaments has to be brought
together and arranged. For the final occasion the process of decoration may
take as much time as is actually spent in dancing. Men begin decorating
themselves in the half-light of early dawn, starting at their own courtyards
and drifting to the ceremonial grounds (Pl. 2) where either they or their helpers

5

attend to the detailed application of face-paint and plumes (Pl. 3). Dancing does not begin till late in the morning and must be over before the afternoon rain, allowing time for the actual transfer of the gifts and for speeches, which are an important part of the whole occasion. For the act of transfer, dancers remove their precious plumes, kilt up their aprons, and rush to lay out the shells or tie up the pigs. (Shells are displayed in rows on the ceremonial ground where the dances take place (Col. pl. 3); pigs are similarly tied to a line of stakes.)

Both those making and those receiving the gifts may dance together on the final day. But it is significant that only the donors are likely to embark on practice dances, for it is their wealth and skills which are primarily under test. Moreover, within the donor group there is a kind of informal division of labour. Older men concentrate on preparations for the gift itself, while younger men become enthusiastic dancers, and carry their exuberance over into courting parties at night. At an earlier stage, the leaders (big-men) may pronounce on the general set of plumes to be worn for the occasion (we discuss these sets in more detail later). Now, while passing by for discussions with exchange partners, they drop into the ceremonial ground in order to criticise the dancers' performance, telling them to keep the line straight, maintain a steady rhythm, or sing more loudly. Women, meanwhile, are kept busy with their everyday tasks. Even if the occasion is one at which they are to take a prominent part, often they dress up only for the final day.

Men who live near by may come fully dressed to the ceremonial ground. Those from further away arrive with their families and sit in little domestic knots while the wife helps the husband with the final preparations. The men regard dancing as something of an ordeal, and expect their wives to bring small pieces of food and gourds of water to sustain them during the day. A brother or an elderly homestead member who is not dancing may help the husband; if a wife is to dance, a sister or cousin or whoever has lent her decorations does the same (Pls 4, 5). Helpers add an additional plume or shell to the women's already heavily draped bodies even as they move into line to begin dancing.

Men don first their large wigs, long aprons, and rear coverings of cordyline leaves. It is with their face-paint and head-dresses that they need most help, although mirrors make the task easier nowadays. Feathers are taken individually from flat storage packs and inserted into the wig or into a softwood support attached to it.

Hageners sometimes say that arranging feathers is men's work, but that wives should help with other details. Wives adjust fresh cordyline sprigs and ferns in their husbands' rear coverings, and anoint them with oil and pig-fat (Col. pl. 8). The wife also makes the fine long dancing apron which it is imperative on

6

Plate 3
Helpers attend to a dancer's head-dress of eagle feathers

Plate 4
A woman may be
decorated by a female
friend or relative

Plate 5
Finishing touches are
put to the face while the
head-dress is built up
(see Plate 7)

many occasions for a man to wear. Men are very reluctant to lend such an item. If his wife will not make one for him, a man must ask a close female relative and reward her for the service.

Wives also help with face-painting. For this, charcoal mixed with fat or water is smoothed on first. Areas where colour is to be applied are left free, although white paint can be placed directly over the charcoal. Paint brushes are made from twigs with soft leaf swabs at the end, which are dipped into the powdered colours (Pl. 6). Throughout the period of practice dances individuals may experiment with slightly different designs; or they may keep to a favourite one. As we shall see, certain broad colour emphases are appropriate to particular kinds of occasion.

When a man is finally ready, he shakes out his apron and his wife straightens it so as to hide the older apron he wears underneath. He moves stiffly into the row of dancers or joins others who are collecting for a ceremonial entry. The newly decorated men parade flamboyantly, whereas when women are dressed up they seem to move with more diffidence and to keep close together in hesitant little knots as they arrive at the ceremonial ground or take up their dancing stations (Pl. 7).

At the end of the dancing men may remove their feathers without much ceremony, yet the act is of some importance. It is called 'I dig out my furs and feathers' (*kui køi ak^end*), and it marks a return to more mundane affairs after the ceremonial period.

When a woman removes her decorations her husband may pay her kin, both in return for their help over the festival time in supplying ornaments and to symbolise the woman's re⁄entry into the role of a working wife.

At the climax of a festival sequence a man will be entertaining many of his relatives, and the presence of visitors is marked by the killing of pigs to provide them with pork. The dancers themselves should also be well looked after, since they are displaying equally their decorations and their own beauty and health. Not only does their attire have to meet the critical appraisal of the other dancers who are anxious to make a good overall impression, but the ceremonial ground is thronged with a crowd of spectators who scrutinise them, sometimes pressing so close to the dance formation that they stand within a few inches of the performers' slanting spears (Col. pl. 1).

Spectators admire a group which shows a measure of conformity in its decorations. Decisions are made early on as to what basic 'set' is to be worn; thereafter, anyone who fails to find at least the main items in the set will be labelled a 'rubbish man'. The overall group effect thus depends on each individual's success in obtaining the requisite decorations.

People not only comment on the general magnificence of a display but also refer to what we would call 'aesthetic' concepts: to the overall appearance of a dancer, and the way the different items of his attire fit together and suit the occasion. These aesthetic judgements are in fact closely related to the symbolism of the decorations, and in the second part of the book we shall attempt to explain this symbolism. Before coming to this, however, we must describe the decorations themselves, and how they are obtained, in more detail. We have mentioned that relatives often lend decorations to each other. We need to understand something of the social system to see how this operates. Moreover, we have indicated that certain sets of decorations are appropriate for particular occasions: we need to know what the sets are, the contexts in which they are worn, and how decisions are made as to which should be put on. And we must consider a complicating factor also: apart from the appropriateness of different assemblages, Hageners are aware that different regions have their own 'styles'. To show this, we begin with a brief description of the problem of cultural areas around Hagen.

The Hagen area takes its name from the 13,000-foot mountain which encloses its western limits. To its east opens out the Wahgi Valley, flanked by ranges to the north and south. Mount Hagen township, administrative centre for the Western Highlands District in the Territory of Australian New Guinea, stands between the Wahgi and Nebilyer Valleys (see map, p. 2).

The Hageners were not discovered by Europeans until the early 1930s, when gold prospectors, Administration patrol officers, and missionaries, aided by light aircraft, first made their way over high ranges into the Wahgi Valley.[1] Mount Hagen became a European centre, and is now a small township with growing numbers of European residents.

Around it, within some 30–40 miles, live roughly 90,000 speakers of two major languages, Melpa (c. 60,000 people, mainly living north of the township) and Gawigl (c. 30,000, living mainly to its south). Speakers of the two languages are very similar in culture and social structure, and we draw our examples from both areas, although we know the Melpa speakers best.

These two languages are closely related, and belong to a family of languages stretching east of Hagen to Chimbu. The dialects of Gawigl are Temboka, Kauil, and Imbonggu, spoken around Tambul, in the Nebilyer Valley, and near to Mount Ialibu respectively. Our term 'Hageners' refers to Melpa and Temboka speakers, excluding the Kauil and Imbonggu further to their south.[2]

The relationship between linguistic and cultural differences in the Highlands is complex. Much depends on which items of custom are considered. If we look at dance decorations alone, it is clear that the Imbonggu head-dress (a kind of top-hat, worn for pig-killing festivals) differs from those of the Melpa and Temboka speakers and resembles head-dresses of the Kewa and Wiru peoples south of Ialibu, who belong to a different language family.[3] If we look at other cultural features, however, the picture becomes more complicated; for example, there are religious cults practised by Temboka speakers in the southern Nebilyer Valley, which are found also among the Imbonggu but are completely unknown to the northern Melpa. There may be conscious borrowings of ceremonial dress between areas which are otherwise sharply different: Hageners (Melpa and Temboka) have adopted a style of ceremonial wig which derives from Enga people to their west. Cults, spells, folk-tales, as well as modes of decoration and dances, appear to have spread across a number of language areas[4] via ceremonial friendships, trade routes, and marriage ties. It would thus be unprofitable for us to attempt to draw complete and unequivocal boundaries round some hypothetical 'Hagen' culture area. The most we can say is that transitions from group to group are more gradual in some directions than in others.

Yet the people themselves do have notions of 'our custom' and 'their custom' which can apply to entities wider than local political groups. And nowadays, at any rate, since the creation of Mount Hagen as a European township, they sometimes speak in terms of 'Hagen custom'. The relative nature of such a concept can easily be shown: in one case, at a dance performed near the territories of Wahgi language speakers to the east (in the Melpa-speaking Kuli area), the dancers regarded themselves as following Hagen ways; but men from nearer the township emphasised that the Kuli were really more like Wahgi Valley men in their decorations. Both the Kuli and our informants were right, with regard to different items of their assemblages: their wigs and aprons and face-painting linked the Kuli to other Melpa speakers, whereas their feather arrangements bore points of resemblance to the Wahgi styles. We shall look at this example in more detail later.

ENVIRONMENT, SOCIAL STRUCTURE, AND VALUES

The Central Highlands consists of wide valleys, more than 5,000 feet in altitude, flanked by heavily forested ranges. In Hagen the main settled valleys are the Nebilyer (Temboka speakers), the western end of the Wahgi (Central Melpa) and the Mᶜka (Northern Melpa). Some Melpa speakers also inhabit the Jimi Valley.

People live in homesteads and hamlets situated both in valley areas and on the ranges. They are agriculturists, growing as a staple crop sweet potatoes, which feed both themselves and their pigs. Men traditionally have separate sleeping houses from their wives and young children. Women's houses include compartments in which pigs come to feed and sleep at night. Men clear and fence gardens, and plant bananas and sugar-cane; women plant and harvest a variety of green crops and the sweet potato. After six to nine months a new planting of sweet potatoes bears its tubers, which are then harvested gradually until the garden is exhausted. Women spend most of their time in the gardens; men have much more time for discussions, visits and making plans for exchange. Moreover, only men are the formal owners of pigs, valuables, and land, although women have strong claims over the use of these. In the past the men were often involved in warfare also. Their time free from subsistence work and fighting must have increased greatly since the ban on warfare and the replacement of stone by introduced steel tools.[5] Men, in fact, gain more from these changes than the women, who still have to harvest food daily with the traditional digging-stick, often in gardens distant from their homes.

Gardening is efficient enough to prevent severe food shortages, although each year there tends to be a lean period of two months or so when old gardens are exhausted and new ones have not yet begun to bear. Weather is drier from

May to September, wetter from October to April, with an overall rainfall of about 100 inches per year, and noon temperatures of over 29 °C. Clearing of gardens proceeds in all but the wettest of times.

There is no single season which is definitely laid aside for festivals, nor do Hagen festivals take the clear cyclical form which is known in other parts of the New Guinea Highlands: Hageners do not emphasise massive pig-killings for which groups must build up their herds over periods of five to seven years.[6] The Hagen *moka* system entails instead a more continuous flow of shell valuables and live pigs, marked from time to time by co-ordinated gifts from one group to others. The result is, as we have already noted, that men may hold or attend more than one *moka* festival in a year, although in some years they will be more active than in others.

Payments of shell valuables and pigs at these occasions are often phrased as compensation for allies or ex-enemies as a result of their losses in past warfare. They are like war indemnities: if an ally group lost a man in fighting on one's behalf, the death should be paid for; similarly with killings between actual enemies, provided they were not major or traditional enemies. In practice these payments lead to reciprocal exchanges between the groups involved, which continue over the years. Exchanges are ostensibly made to keep the peace; but they contain a latent rivalry, expressed in the size of gifts, in speeches, and in decorations themselves. Religious cults also provide occasions for the transfer of wealth.

The political unit most often involved in payments and cult performances is one of perhaps 50–100 men, who live, with their wives and children, within a common territory. We call this unit a clan. Clansmen emphasise their unity by declaring that they are descended from an original male ancestor, their 'one father'. Clan membership is obtained by a variety of means, most often through one's father. A clan is exogamous: members may not marry within it. At marriage women are expected to move to their husband's settlement, although variation is allowed here: women may refuse to go, husbands and in-laws can stay with their affines, and so on. At festivals, clansmen dance as a single group, but they may be joined by other kinsmen and by whole clans of 'helpers' who swell the line of dancers.

Each clan consists of smaller units, described as 'men's house groups',[7] which have some autonomy in exchange relations, especially if they include someone who is a big-man; and clans themselves are segments of tribes. Tribes range from fewer than 500 to over 6,000 people (counting wives and children as well as men). Within a tribe clans are often paired together, each pair being regular allies in exchange (and for warfare in the past). Individuals of each clan also have links through their mothers, wives, and sisters with outside clans,

14

Plate 7 Fully decorated women arriving at the ceremonial ground

and these links are used for exchange partnerships.

Particularly prominent for their extra-clan ties are the clan leaders. Their influence depends on success in exchange and oratory. To raise valuables for use in exchange they must mobilise both their home resources and supporters from inside and outside their clan. Wives are important here for men in two ways: they raise pigs and they provide links with other groups. Hence it is an advantage for an aspiring leader to be a polygynist. In addition, leaders can make partnerships with unrelated friends in both neighbouring and distant groups. They are said pre-eminently to 'attract' wealth to themselves, and their success is to some extent taken as the success of their clan also. Their aim is to 'win' by attracting more wealth than other men or other groups are able to do. This point is relevant to our theme, since the actual decorations worn at dances are held to increase one's chances of 'winning' by making their wearers more attractive to exchange partners and to potential wives also. Decorations are thought of as magically 'pulling in' valuables and women.

One of the ways in which an important man demonstrates his ability to influence others is by taking charge of the planning and timing of exchange festivals. Timing can be a matter for dispute, since all the participants are under pressure to raise resources to a maximum and not everyone is ready at the same juncture. Men have to find decorations to wear as well as valuables to give away, and this complicates their preparations. Big-men among the donors, as we have noted, pronounce on the general styles their groups will wear, and recipients and 'helpers' adjust their styles accordingly. One of the functions of the practice dances is to communicate, both within the dancing group and to others, the kinds of decorations being assembled and the degree of preparedness of the donors. While an overall effect of uniformity is aimed at, individuals are free to choose many of the minor items which they will wear (cf. Col. pls 4, 13). In fact, much depends on which items they can obtain from friends and relatives. Big-men do not dictate all details of the decorations; nor do they have a prerogative over particular items (except for certain occasions, which we describe later). Since, however, they are wealthy, they may be in a better position than others to acquire the necessary ornaments.

To sum up the points which are important for us here: the people have sufficient food surpluses to support pigs, which are one of the bases of wealth; and they have enough time free from subsistence work to engage in elaborate ceremonies and religious cults. Their exchange system is not rigidly tied to a cycle of stock-production but operates through a variety of financial arrange-ments. Men have more free time than women, and they are the principal dancers and transactors; but they depend on women for pig-production and for many of their exchange ties. Periodic displays and gifts of wealth mediate relations between big⁄men and between clans, highlighting both links and rivalries. It is at these displays that formal sets of decorations are worn. What decorations the participants actually wear is partly a result of big⁄men's pronouncements, but it also depends on individual effort and choice. Success in acquiring ornaments is felt to parallel and to indicate the general prosperity of the individual and his clan.

CHAPTER TWO

Decorations and how they are obtained

THE ITEMS OF DECORATION

Many decorations are themselves valuables, used in exchanges. Other items, although not major valuables, must be obtained through trade or hunting, or be borrowed for a particular dance.

The most important traditional items are shells, plumes and furs, wigs and aprons. Accessories are: drums, weapons, bones, oil and pig-grease, cane, vines, leaves, grasses, and earth paints. Nowadays trade-store paints, cloth and beads are included.

Obtaining such articles involved (and still partly involves) the Hageners in a nexus of trading relations which spread out well beyond their own language area.[1] Shells, for example, traditionally came along trade routes from the Southern Highlands and the Wahgi Valley, and were exchanged for pigs, stone axes, packs of native salt, and long bamboo tubes of decorating oil. These latter came to Hagen from as far away as Lake Kutubu in Papua. Salt and axes were produced only in specific, scattered parts of the Highlands:[2] the use of shells and pigs as currency facilitated the dispersal of these items, needed for subsistence, over a wide area. Men travelled in small parties to their trade-friends (who might also be relatives) and obtained the items they needed on an individual basis. Trade was organised through interpersonal networks, not through markets.

The restrictions on obtaining other raw materials for decoration – i.e. plumes, furs, and plants – are those which limit access to clan hunting-grounds. Only

Plate 8
Informal decoration of
cassowary topknot (see pl. 23)
parrot wings and nassa
shell band

some groups have good access to forest areas, and others must depend on kin-links with them for a share in forest products. But clans rarely have an overall advantage. For example, Jimi Valley clans have good hunting-grounds and in the past exploited stone axe quarries also; but they were further away from the trade routes in shell and salt than other Hagen groups. All groups depended on the circulation of shells and this carried the minor decorative items with it.

Shells, in fact, had a wide use as currency in the past, although they are now partly replaced by Australian money. Besides their employment in *moka* and in bridewealth, they could be used to purchase magic (either spells or in the form of stones held to have magical power), poison, paints, services of ritual experts, and hired killers; and in compensation for insults, injuries, and killings, as well as for certain obligatory life-cycle payments to maternal kin.[3] What is interesting for us here is that the value of shells was at least partly based on an appreciation of their brightness or iridescent gleam (Col. pl. 2). It is this quality which pleases the Hageners' eye, and which, they say, makes shells also good for decorations. Moreover, the brightness is itself held magically to attract further wealth. This supposed attribute of brightness becomes important to our later argument.

The individual types of shell[4] are: pearl shell, worn either as a crescent (Col. pl. 9) or mounted on a board of hardened resin (Col. pl. 13); bailer, worn in a cut-down form on the forehead or in a fuller curved form over the chest (Pl. 7); conus, suspended from the pierced nasal septum (Pl. 7) (slivers of pearl shell or bone can be inserted in the same way); cowries (Pl. 7), now out of fashion, but in the past made up into long ropes or necklaces; green-snail pieces, with their delicate curve and elusive glitter, worn hanging from the ears or hair (Pls 10, 79); and tiny nassa shells, sewn on to bark-cloth and used either as forehead ornaments (Pl. 8) or as larger mats draped from the waist – like cowries, they are now rather out of fashion.

Pearl shells, in particular, are felt to be enhanced by the way they are mounted. They are backed with pandanus leaves and set into a prepared board of tree resin. The resin is softened with a heated stone or piece of iron, and sets hard over the shell's edge. Red ochre paint is sprinkled freshly over the board each time the shell is displayed. Decorating the shells is felt to parallel the way men decorate and paint themselves (Pl. 9).

Before Europeans came, shells were all scarce. Only an important man would possess many, obtained through his extensive exchange contacts. But European prospectors, Government officers, missionaries and planters all brought in large numbers to pay for labour and food, and they soon inflated the currency. Cowries and nassa bands eventually went out of circulation as currency, and have since lost much of their popularity as ornaments also.

Bailers have lost their currency function, but are retained as forehead and chest decorations.[5] Previously, also, shells had entered the Hagen area ready-cut and shaped. Europeans, however, brought them in uncut condition, and Hageners had to scrape, cut, and bore them themselves.

The influx of shells brought with it another change. In the past, when pearl shells were scarcer, women used to make carefully stitched handles for them; but now the men took to attaching rough handles of cloth or sacking. In the past, too, each shell was named, and bore a knotted rope tally of the number of times it had changed hands. Decorative marsupial teeth hung from the tally. Nowadays the tallies have been abandoned and only the largest and finest shells are named.[6]

Plumes are also traded, and in the past circulated as items for bridewealth payments. Many of the birds whose plumage is valued live only in forest habitats, and men from the grasslands of the Wahgi have to trade for them (paying shells and Australian money) or obtain them through kin ties. Parrots, cockatoos, and cassowaries (Pls 8, 10) are most commonly found in the Jimi Valley. The Red and White birds of paradise[7] (Col. pls 8, 22) sometimes

Plate 9
Inside a men's house red ochre is smoothed over pearl shell mounts

21

frequent copses near to settlements, where they can be shot. More often, men go into the forest to shoot them. The hunter may aim at birds while they feed on fruit trees or drink at streams. Or he builds himself a shelter in a tree where birds of paradise display, and ensconces himself there overnight till they arrive in the morning.[8]

Only men and boys hunt for birds and marsupials. The marsupial hunter waits for a moonlit night and takes a boy with him to cook food while he searches. He hopes to shoot his prey with pronged arrows or to find it caught in a noose he has set along a branch.

Plumes are worth as much as $A10 or $A20; furs $A1 or 50 cents.

Like the plumes and furs, many of the leaves and grasses worn as accessories come from forest areas and are collected by males. Before dances there are special excursions to obtain them. A few leaves are picked from planted shrubs: one favourite (Euphorbiaceae *Croton* sp.) has a glossy, mottled yellow and green colour (Pl. 11). Another is cordyline, which appears in green, red, wine-black, and red and yellow combinations. Ordinary green cordylines belong especially to men. They form men's usual rear-coverings, and they also mark out ceremonial grounds and settlement areas. Red and multicoloured cordylines demarcate internal divisions between garden strips worked by separate women, and are correspondingly planted and worn mainly by women and girls. Men use small, soft ferns as appendages to their beards (Pl. 11, Col. pl. 14). Silver-grey and rusty-brown leaves, together with another type of fern,[9] appear in all kinds of ritual contexts, associated with ancestral skulls, men's houses, and male cults. Appropriately, only men wear them.

Flowers play a relatively unimportant part in decoration. They are worn only as a part of casual attire, not formally at the major festivals (Col. pl. 27). Nowadays they are popular, as adornments for the hair and for bangles worn on the upper arm, among girls of courting age.

There is a special significance in the fact that many of the valued plumes, furs, and leaves come from the forest. The forest is the domain of wild spirits, and hunting there is essentially an intrusion by men. Success in hunting is thought to depend on the favour of ancestral ghosts, who intercede with the wild spirits to allow the men to catch their prey.[10] The ancestors also help men in the actual wearing of plumes and furs, for it is they who are thought to make decorations bright.

Wigs and aprons contrast with the items we have been concerned with so far: they are usually made locally, by the dancers or their close relatives. A man's wig consists largely of his own hair, and although others may help him in its construction, it is too personal an object to lend to someone else. We have already mentioned that men depend on their wives or female relatives for

Plate 10
Lorikeet, parrot,
cockatoo among the
feathers of a girl's
head-dress

making aprons. These may be borrowed to a limited extent. Men more often borrow the 'pig's tail aprons', to be described later, which are worn on relatively few occasions and tend to be scarce; but a man may be embarrassed if he has to go to another to borrow one of the ordinary long dancing aprons.

We give further details of wigs and aprons in chapter four, where we also describe styles of head-dresses. Here we look rather more briefly at other accessory items.

a. *Weapons*: only men make these and only men hold them at dances. Spears with carved hooks as a centre-piece also have marsupial fur bound decoratively round them (Pl. 33). Plain spears have white paint, mixed with resin to harden it, applied to a foot or so of their length near the tip, or they may simply be rubbed with grease. Arrow-heads, pushed into a hollow cane shaft, have a woven circlet and a tuft of marsupial fur bound over the join.

b. *Ceremonial axes*: especially fine stone axes are held at dances, displayed at a slight distance from the dancers' bodies (nowadays, steel axes and even hammers or chisels are sometimes employed in this way). The present-day stone axes are often made for European tourists to buy.[11] In the past they had little clusters of bamboo rings attached to them, the plaiting on the haft covered a smaller area than on modern specimens, and the blades were of a markedly finer quality[12] (Pl. 57).

Fresh leaves and grasses may be tied to all these weapons. Like pearl shells they are both themselves decorated and become decorations when held by a dancer.

Shields are also ornamented but are never held in dancing at festivals. (We describe how they are decorated in chapter four.)

c. *Bones*: men wear cassowary leg-bone spatulae protruding from their wigs on either side of the face (Pls 8, 11). They also insert curved pig-tusks into the pierced septum. (Wooden pins, feathers and cassowary quills may also be worn in this position, the latter especially by unmarried girls.)

d. *Grease*: both men and women rub their bodies with grease to make them shine. Liquid pig-fat is scooped into bamboo tubes and gourd flasks when cooked pork is removed from the earth ovens. Oil is also squeezed from red and yellow pandanus fruits (*Pandanus conoideus*). Tree-oil traded from Kutubu[13] is the substance most prized for anointing the skin: one name for it is 'face good grease'.

e. *Cane and vines*: the best cane is procured from the Jimi Valley. Men split and bend canes round their bark belts (Pl. 57); they may incise them lightly and polish them as well. Another type of cane is woven into ornaments also for their belts, or to go round their arms (Pl. 4). Sometimes orchid vines

Plate 11
Croton leaves fringe the pale marsupial fur, ferns the beard

are twisted together to make a bright yellow armband. (In the past men wore legbands and women wristbands plaited from rope fibre.)

f. *Drums:* these are hollowed out by fire and carved to an hour-glass shape (Pl. 32, Col. pl. 5). They may have furs decorating the marsupial skin tympanum, and perhaps some patterned incisions on the rest of their surface, filled at festival times with paint. Individuals usually make their own; drums do not circulate widely. Perhaps a fifth of the performers at a dance bring drums, and these provide the main musical accompaniment.

g. *Earth paints:* white, blue or yellow clays are apparently found easily enough, often in and beside rivers. As pigments, they are used in powdered form. The material from which red ochre powder is produced is scarcer, because it is found only in a few sites; further, the powder has a wider range of uses than the other pigments: as well as decorating pearl shell boards, for example, it is wrapped up in bark-cloth packs with stones kept for magical purposes. The reason for these special uses is the association which Hageners make between red ochre and health-cum-wealth. Thus a sanction on decorating pearl shells is that if ochre is not sprinkled over them their owner will die.[14] Again, many of the 'magic stones' are kept specifically in order to attract pigs and shells to their owners, and red ochre is held to increase their effectiveness. It is especially spoken of as 'bright' in colour.

The raw material for red ochre is a rusty-brown clay. Manufacturers wrap quantities of the clay in wild asparagus leaves (Pl. 12), and bake it on a wooden trestle over a fire, turning the packs with tongs. After an hour or so the fire dies down. They break the clay open and, blowing on the particles to remove the ash and to make them glow, lay them on a bed of banana leaves (Pl. 13). The reddest portions inside are crumbled to use as pigment (Pl. 14).

Anyone local to the area where the requisite clay is found can obtain the raw material: it is the work of manufacture which is paid for when it is traded. The skill required for making it is not a specialised one; and we may remark in general that although skill enters the construction of other items, such as spears and shields, Hageners lay no great emphasis on technological expertise or craftsmanship. The one area in which specialist skill is recognised is in the making of particular types of wig,[15] and even here the specialists do not gain high social status because of their skills. It is the ability to *acquire* beautiful objects – through purchase or borrowing, both of which indicate influence over people – which brings prestige.[16]

Plate 12
The wet clay is wrapped in leaves

Plate 13
Ochre extracted from the ashes: to bring out its colour bright red leaves are placed in the banana-leaf receptacle

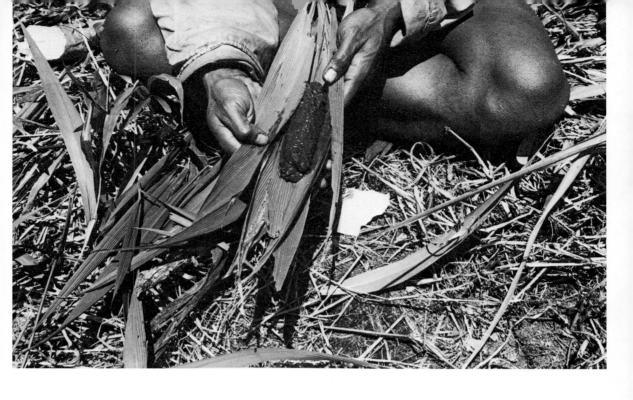

Most men own some shells and plumes, but for a dance they may need to borrow many items. It is this fact which provides one of the incentives for the creation of wide trade and friendship networks.

It is only the mounted pearl shells which are nowadays used as major exchange valuables. Men obtain them in sets of eight or ten through the *moka* system, and also in ones and twos as individual gifts, by purchase in trade stores, through distribution of bridewealth payments, and so on. Mounted shells can be worn as ornaments also, by their owners themselves or by the owners' womenfolk. Other types of shell, including the unmounted pearl shell crescent, as we have seen, are now confined to use as decorations. A man who borrows such an item, however, both returns it to its owner and pays for the borrowing as well.

Men store shells and good feathers in their men's houses, packed in card-board and paper (previously in bark-cloth and pandanus leaves). Second-best feather assemblages can simply be hung up in an outhouse, where fires are not often lit, so they do not become besmirched. Women should not step over men's feathers, for it is thought that a woman's polluting influence would make them lose their brightness. This taboo falls into line with others which separate male activities from females: for example, with rules forbidding men to have inter-course when they make shields and spears, since to do so would render the weapons weak; and more generally with rules which protect men from menstruating women. Women, none the less do sometimes wear feathers, and on these occasions they decorate themselves even more elaborately and brightly than the men. This apparent paradox we examine later.

Although plumes are wealth objects, they are not circulated regularly in ceremonial exchanges as pigs and pearl shells are, nor do big-men make special efforts to accumulate them. Nevertheless, they are perhaps the most important category of decorations and in the remainder of this section we concentrate on them, to give a closer idea of the numbers which men own and the numbers they have to borrow for a dance occasion.

We asked men from two tribes (Elti and Kawelka) what feathers they currently possessed, either as sets or single plumes, depending on how the feathers are worn (Table 1).

The Red bird is clearly the one most commonly owned, followed by eagle, palm cockatoo, King of Saxony, Blue bird, and cassowary. The last are popular as 'second-best' feathers, worn for visits to other groups' festivals. The other most frequently owned types are all important for *moka* decorations. The *køi wal* are important also, but fewer men possess them, and they are regularly borrowed for dances.

There are minor differences between the two groups. Blue birds are more easily obtained by the Kawelka (Northern Melpa), for the Elti (Central Melpa) lack immediate access to forest areas. However, a preponderance of particular feathers can be as much a matter of local popularity as of special

TABLE I: *Ownership of feathers*

Type of bird	Latin term	Melpa term	Elti men owning this type (out of 40 men)	Kawelka men (out of 30)
1. King of Saxony	*Pteridophora alberti* (Meyer)	ketepa	8	12
2. Red parrot (*Eclectus*)	*Lorius roratus?*	puklør	11	4
3. Palm cockatoo?	*Prosciger aterrimus*	kumin	18	9
4. Red bird of paradise	*Paradisaea raggiana* (Sclater)	parka	27	29
5. Harpyopsis eagle	*Harpyopsis novaeguineae* (Salvadori)	ndoa	13	14
6. White bird of paradise	*Paradisaea minor* (Shaw)	kuri	0	4
7. Blue bird of paradise	*Paradisaea rudolphi* (Finsch)	mang	6	12
8. Black sickle-billed bird of paradise	*Epimachus fastosus* ⎫	rumba	3	1
Brown sickle-billed bird of paradise	*Epimachus mayeri* ⎭			
9. Princess Stephanie's bird of paradise	*Astrapia stephaniae* (Finsch & Mayer)	mek	2	0
10. Mountain cassowary	*Casuarius bennetti* (Gould)	raema	6	12
11. Composite of feathers set on backing	—	køi wal	5	7

Notes to Table 1

Our sources for the English and Latin terms are: Cayley 1963; Rand and Gilliard 1967. The list does not include all the birds whose plumage is worn, but it covers most of those commonly used in decorations. Three which were not enquired about are the Superb bird of paradise (*Lophorina superba*, Melpa *klønt*), the Sulphur-crested white cockatoo (*Kakatöe galerita*, Melpa *atekla* or *konmba*), and the Ribbon-tailed astrapia (*Astrapia mayeri* (Stoner), Melpa *kuklup*). Hybrids of types 4 and 6 have more or less pronounced yellow colours in their tail plumes. Our 'equations' of ornithological with Melpa terms should be taken as only approximate. All the Melpa terms are prefixed in ordinary usage by *køi* (which includes bats and flying foxes as well as birds). *Køi wal* means 'a bag of birds', i.e. various kinds of plumage stitched together (Col. pl. 7).

access to hunting-grounds. Thus, neither the Elti nor the Kawelka possess many of the long, black, Sicklebill and Princess Stephanie feathers, although the latter, at least, can hunt these in their own territory. Northern Melpa men in fact prefer to trade these plumes for the high prices which Wahgi and Chimbu travellers will pay for them, rather than retaining them for their own head-dresses.

Only fourteen of the seventy men owned five or more different types of feathers (of those we inquired about). Four of the fourteen were big-men in the two groups. Big-men often expect to lend a few feathers to supporters, and in general it is possible for men to borrow from other clansmen who have more than they themselves need. But there is also rivalry within a clan to procure the best feathers, and men turn to their extra-clan connections for loans of plumes, repaying their helpers with pork at a special cooking just before the dance. Thus, while all the clansmen wear similar decorations and dance as a unit, each man's assemblage is obtained individually through his own extra-clan ties.

Pigs cooked to pay for decorations are called 'pigs for the bird's quill', a

Plate 14
The quality of the colour is tried out

reference to the cassowary quills which support sprays of Saxony feathers worn by donors at a *moka* (Col. pl. 9). Wearing these feathers is particularly closely associated with making *moka*, and the pigs are thought of as cooked especially to pay for them. In the past there was also a sacrifice to clan ancestors, and a ritual performed by an expert, both undertaken to ensure that the feathers would be bright. European missions have forbidden these customs.

Besides paying for their own decorations, men may be paying for those of their wives and unmarried daughters as well, if it is one of the rather rare occasions when women may dance in full decorations. As we have mentioned, they also entertain numbers of relatives and friends. Some of the visitors are those who have supplied feathers; others may bring food or pigs or shells to help their hosts make *moka*; others again come simply to receive meat and to watch the dancing. At one pig-cooking,[17] out of 137 visitors entertained by one clan only about a third brought feathers, food, or valuables. The most numerous guests were in-laws and married sisters (86), and of these 63 came without contributions; but they would expect to reciprocate in kind later by playing host whenever their own group danced for a *moka*. Incidentally, the amount of meat each person receives is not large; but Hageners are short of protein, and, just as importantly, they like visiting kinsfolk and taking part in the excitement of festivals. The hosts also welcome large numbers of guests. Provided the *moka* goes well, the visitors will spread the story of the occasion and increase the group's renown.

Festivals demand particular kinds of feathers, as we have noted, and dancers must shoot, buy, or borrow them if they do not possess them already. We show the pattern of acquisition of plumes for one cult festival[18] which requires both White and Red bird of paradise feathers (Table 2).

TABLE 2: *Acquisition of plumes for a cult festival*

	White plumes	Red plumes
1. Shot by owner (either for the occasion or earlier)	9	2
2. Bought for the occasion	6	3
3. Loaned or given outright:		
a. by an in-law	6	12
b. by a kinsman	19	11
c. by a friend	5	—
	45	28

Shot or bought: 20   Loaned or given: 53
Category 3a and b.
Number of plumes obtained from:

i. in-laws of own generation	16
ii. senior in-laws	2
iii. clanmates	16
iv. extra-clan kin	14
	48

Most of the plumes were thus borrowed or obtained as special gifts. Extra-clan connections provided thirty-seven out of fifty-three plumes. White bird feathers are quite easily found in the area where the cult performers live, since they are close to immense tracts of the bird's forest habitat – by contrast with the two groups whose ownership of feathers we presented earlier. (Only four men in Table 1 owned White bird feathers.) But no group possesses a monopoly over plumes, and differential access to them is not made a basis of organised trading. As we have stressed before, trade and borrowing take place according to individual needs and the requirements of particular occasions.

Men's ability to obtain items of decoration, through whatever channels, demonstrates their individual skill; while the net display which results from their efforts shows the strength of their group *vis-à-vis* its rivals.

CHAPTER THREE

Informal and formal decoration

The most important occasions on which decorations are worn are formal ones, when dancers display themselves publicly before spectators; and our main interest is in these formal occasions. But ornaments are also worn for less formal affairs, and people often casually decorate themselves in their everyday activities. However, if we look at the contexts in which informal decorations are worn, we find that many of them reveal elements of display and ceremonial which link them to the more formal ones.

Hageners say that they decorate themselves for everyday affairs, courting parties, warfare, religious cults, and exchange festivals. Only the latter two are said to merit important decorations. The Melpa term which we represent here as 'decoration' is *moke*. It refers to the whole process of wearing special clothing, plumes, grasses, shells, and so on, and to carrying accessories such as spears and axes. A second word, *waep*, refers to painting of designs, particularly on the face.

The only major occasion at which decorations are inappropriate is a funeral. Mourning behaviour is in some ways the opposite to that of festivals. For example, at festivals men and women don wigs, paint their faces, and grease their bodies; when mourning they tear off their wigs, smear mud or clay over the body and face, and may be covered in ashes as well (Pls 15, 16): mud and ashes make the skin 'bad' and 'dry', which is the reverse of the effect desired in applying grease. Mourners also tear out their hair (Pl. 17); old men (cf. Pl. 18) sometimes wear their hair permanently unkempt and un-bewigged from grief for a dead son.

Plate 15
Mourner plastered with
yellow clay

Smearing mud and ashes over the body is not regarded as 'decorating'
(*moke*) at all, for decorating always implies the attempt of a person to make
himself more impressive and attractive. The situation with regard to warfare
is interesting here. For warfare, decorations were put on, but fights could easily
result in death and mourning, and this seems reflected in ambiguous attitudes
to war ornaments themselves.

We can make a rough scheme of contexts, ranging from those in which
least decoration is worn to those in which it is most elaborate. We should

34

Plate 16
Women at the funeral of a
big-man

Plate 17
Men tear at their hair in
grief

Plate 18
Old men may not bother
to cover their hair

emphasise, before describing these in more detail, that not everyone wears the same amount of decoration, especially in everyday affairs. Variations in the precise items chosen and their arrangements seem, in fact, to be a way of expressing individuality. Our account simply indicates the kinds of items from which people are expected to choose their assemblages.

Plate 19
A neat wig is worn for visiting, trimmed with fur and leaves

Plate 20
The long *omak* of a big-man

INFORMAL OCCASIONS

For ordinary garden work or jobs round the house little attention is paid to clothing. Men wear a bark belt, with an old string apron in front and leaves behind; their heads may be uncovered. Women's regular wear, besides a long, corded genital apron, is a large string netbag suspended from the forehead and hanging over the back. It is a mark of correct behaviour in women to wear a covering of this kind for their head and back.[1] In their netbags women carry up to fifty pounds of food and perhaps a baby as well.

36

Women, as we noted in the first chapter, spend much more time on household tasks than do men. Hageners speak of them as staying at home to work, while their husbands walk about visiting and obtaining valuables. Correspondingly, men are much more likely to decorate themselves: they wear ornaments to impress their friends and get the wealth items they want. It is rather the same with young girls, who are expected to visit places away from their own settle ments to attend courting parties: their decorations are put on to impress potential husbands and to attract a good bridewealth payment. The daughters of big men are likely to be those most adorned.

When they smarten themselves up, men first pay attention to their hair, putting on a wig covered with a knitted head net (Pl. 11), trimmed with grass and leaves (Pl. 19), perhaps a marsupial fur and a topknot of old feathers. Nowadays a bright handkerchief frequently replaces the fur. Boys some times wear flowers in place of feathers. Round the neck men suspend a pearl shell or a set of bamboo tally sticks (omak), which indicate how many times they have given away sets of eight or ten shells in moka[2] (Pl. 20). Fresh cordyline leaves are stuck in the rear of their bark belt.

Pearl shell pendants are the commonest form of ornament for women, given to them by their fathers, brothers or husbands[3] (Pl. 21). Younger women, newly married or still unmarried, wear trade store bangles and beads as armlets and necklaces (Pl. 24). Courting girls amass rows of bead necklaces, given to them mainly by senior kinsfolk, but also partly by boys as favours. They wear bright trade cloth as a cloak over the back, where an older woman has a traditional net covering or an old blanket.

For visiting, girls may in addition put a little grease or oil on their foreheads, while men may blacken their faces (Pl. 39). Both sexes wear good aprons – men choose ones that are ample and not ragged with age; women and girls wear specially oiled and blackened ones. Men usually add feathers, or perhaps a tall marsupial tail (Pl. 22), to their wig. A standard type of second best plume is the cassowary, worn either as a cropped pompom (Pl. 23) ot in a larger form in which the plumes spray and trail out (Pl. 28). It is suitable for some formal occasions, too, if men lack the right kinds of 'best' feathers. Visitors at a moka who come simply to watch should also wear cassowary or some other second best type of feather. It goes regularly with a charcoaled, but not otherwise painted, face.

Most often visits are connected with moka or bridewealth exchanges, or with trading. Frequently such 'trading' is subsumed under a kin relationship. Northern Melpa men, for example, visit kinsmen in the Jimi Valley, in order to obtain special forest products as well as decorations. The Jimi men also catch and rear cassowaries, which have been hatched wild in the forest, and exchange

these with their kinsmen for shells, money, pigs and tree-oil. Live cassowaries are an important valuable, used as bridewealth and *moka* gifts. In cash terms, an adult bird is worth about $A100; a chick some $A10.

For courting parties there is more overt emphasis on decoration than for visiting (except for visits at times of festivals). The parties are held regularly, at night-time, in women's houses. Unmarried girls and youths from about fifteen onwards, and also young married men, take part as protagonists. Especially when a new women's house is built, girls and men are invited to come and sing in it, as a kind of house-warming. At least one older married woman acts as chaperone, greeting the men as they arrive, stirring up the fire and watching the performance. Often, there are further spectators, married folk and younger boys, who join in the singing. The girls at first stay in a back compartment of the house, while the men sing romantic songs in a loud, nasal voice, to attract them out. At length the girls emerge and kneel at one end of the room, while two men sit cross-legged on either side of each one. After waving their heads

38

Plate 21
Father and daughter: she has a pearl shell crescent at her neck

Plate 22
Decorated for a courting party

in a stylised preliminary motion, partners press noses together, duck heads down while turning on to the cheek, swing back, turn their heads together twice, retaining contact on the nose and forehead, then duck again. This is the 'turn-head'[4] movement. A girl 'turns' alternately with partners on either side of her. Men replace each other in relays. Courting is supposed to continue till daylight, when the girls have a right to chase their partners out, threatening them with mud and stinging nettles. If a man turns head with a favourite girl several times, he should give her beads, feathers, furs, knives, or money as a compliment; and such gifts can be a preliminary to bridewealth payments.

Men display little overt concern with success at courting parties. Despite their obvious enjoyment of turning-head and their interest in sex, men sometimes say that it is a 'rubbish' activity. One reason may be that courting is neither a necessary nor a sufficient means of obtaining a bride, since marriages are often arranged by senior kin and must be accompanied by bridewealth payments. Another may be that prowess in courting does not of itself bring

Plate 23
'Second-best' ornaments include the cassowary pompom

Plate 24
Talcum powder adds to the effect of flowers in the hair

39

high status, as prowess in exchange does. It is significant that men claim they do not pray to family ghosts to help them in courting, and that courting decorations are not so elaborate as those for *moka*. Nevertheless, they are keen to wear some feathers and furs for turning-head.

For a big party, men and youths gather forest leaves and grasses; for a smaller occasion they simply pick greenery near to their houses. They can wear a variety of feathers: Red bird, eagle, black cassowary, cockatoo, hawk's wing. They can partly charcoal or paint their faces, rub grease on their bodies, insert shells in the nose, and bind marsupial fur round the forehead. All kinds of leaves and grasses (perhaps twenty kinds are regularly used) fringe the beard and wig. Shreds of coloured paper from tin-labels are nowadays popular as topknots. These accessories are worn for the pleasant swishing sound they make as the wearer sways his head. But the feathers should not be too fine, men say, for they are spoilt by fire-smoke and by rubbish on the floor. They add that it is not worthwhile decorating too well for an event that occurs at night, when people cannot see properly. This remark underlines the point that dancing and decorations are intended primarily for public display, hence the major occasions take place in large, cleared spaces and during the daytime.

For turning-head, girls may wear a pearl shell crescent between their breasts, cowrie necklaces and beads, all of which they cover with trade-cloth cloaks knotted in front. They oil their hair, charcoal their foreheads or paint them with a red band, put multicoloured spots or triangles of paint on their cheeks. Girls are supposed to mix love-magic with their pigments and men to do the same with their grease. Such magic is meant to attract the opposite sex by its perfume, and nowadays trade-store scent and talcum powder are used by both sexes for the same purpose. Men can also wear leaves of the resin-bearing *kilt* tree (Rutaceae *Evodiella* sp.),[5] which they invoke in charms to make them attractive. Girls tend not to wear so many leaves and grasses as men, though they often tuck flowers in the hair as a fringe for the forehead (Pl. 24).

Although men usually dress a little more elaborately for courting than girls, in the past a big-man might decorate a young female relative for a courting party with some care, giving her white marsupial fur and a nassa shell band for her brow, and a fine head-dress of brown cassowary feathers. This would be done with a view to sharing in the subsequent bridewealth obtained at her marriage.

Girls may also be permanently tattooed. Designs are usually (though not always) confined to the face, and they resemble those applied with ochre and trade-store paints, although we do not know if they are called by special names as the latter are. Most commonly they consist of dots over the forehead or arching over the eyebrows, and under-eye dots or short streaks at the top of the cheek

Plate 25
Attending a bridewealth:
note the oiled and painted
forehead

Plate 26
Girls dressed for an
occasion such as a
bridewealth or courtin
party

(Pl. 75). Tattoo marks are made by pricking the skin and rubbing in charcoal and blue dye. A mother may tattoo her young daughter; or a man his wife's sister (no doubt other relatives and friends may perform this service also).[6]

Occasions at which bridewealth payments are made are much more elaborate public affairs than courting parties, but are not marked by noticeably more elaborate decorations. The main exchanges between the kin of the bride and groom take place in two stages.[7] First, the groom's sub-clan mates, headed by his father, display live pigs, mounted pearl shells, and money to the bride's kin. Discussion centres on those items which are to be exchanged for equivalents provided by the bride's people. Male participants at this stage rarely bother to decorate themselves. They discuss the 'deal' in a small courtyard at the groom's place.

Although many of the items are for direct exchange the bride's kin hope that a large initial bridewealth will be offered, for this will make a better display at the more public second stage; and to this end they decorate the girl with shells and cook a pig with prayers to the ancestors before sending her to the groom's settlement at the stage of the overtures. They take grease from this pig to rub her with so that her body gleams and appears healthy, and they divine by the way fat drips over her forehead whether the bridewealth will be good or not.[8] The custom reveals an association between bodily appearance, grease, and the ability to attract valuables which we shall find again later.

At the second stage the groom's kinsmen cook further pigs and take them to the bride's place, for display and formal presentation to her kin at the same time as the exchange of shells and live pigs. For the last part of the journey the bride is ceremonially laden with most of the meat and carries it over to her people, who await the visitors at a ceremonial ground. (Her folk later distribute the meat to segments of her clan and to clusters of other kin and in-laws.) Both sides wish to make a good impression on their new friends: men wear second-best feathers, striped possum tails, furs or clean handkerchiefs round their foreheads, fresh cordylines, and a decent apron, and they may oil their skins. Married women may have a new piece of cloth; and marriageable girls dress in the same way as for courting parties, their faces stippled with bright paint, perhaps leaves tucked in their armbands (Pls 25, 26). The bride decorates herself as the girls do, but also dons a large netbag as a sign of her impending work as a married woman. The groom, if this is his first marriage, is not likely to play a prominent part in the proceedings nor is he especially decorated.

Men make speeches on either side when the meat is handed over and the exchanges of wealth are announced. But the occasion does not require full-scale competitive displays by whole clans such as occur at festivals. Perhaps this is why it is not marked by elaborate self-decoration. We could express the point by saying that bridewealth occasions fall half-way between the domestic and the political spheres of action. Other events also, at which a similar range of decorations is worn, fall into the same category. These events are: preliminary meetings for *moka* festivals, special work occasions, Local Government Council meetings and elections, and market days.

Preliminary debates to a *moka* are numerous and lengthy. Sometimes they take place between a few men inside their houses, sometimes more men are present and discussions are held at ceremonial grounds. Prominent leaders deliver speeches, often accompanying their arguments with more or less good-humoured taunts. Donors eventually make overt promises by setting up sticks to represent pigs they will give. Finally, they hold a 'showing' of all the pigs to be transferred, ideally at a single ceremonial ground, as a sign that they are ready for the festival.

Spectators do not attend these preliminaries to a *moka* and women have no part in them.

Special work occasions sometimes involve something closer to public competition between clans than is evinced at bridewealths and *moka* preliminaries, and the competition is accompanied by a greater emphasis on decorations. The work involved is usually the pulling of huge tree-trunks for bridge-building and the cutting of new road sections.[9] It is especially when a home group invites one of its traditionally allied clans to help it that excitement rises. The two groups vie with each other to heave a trunk or complete a section of road. Women and girls may come as spectators, painted and greased as for a dance. Men march to work in ranks holding long-handled spades, like warriors with spears, and may wear decorations close in style to those appropriate for *moka* (Pl. 27).

At one work party, for example, several men had painted their faces with charcoal, and added outlines in white round the eyes, nose, or mouth (Pls 28, 29). They wore various types of feather, predominantly cassowary plumes. At another occasion we took some details of 50 men's decorations. We divided the items into six categories: leaves and grasses, paint and charcoal, feathers, fur, shells, and additional miscellanea. We found that 14 men wore items from four or more categories, 36 from three or fewer. The 50 workers had 23 different combinations of the categories. Despite an overall impression of uniformity, no two men were decorated exactly alike.

Elections,[10] council meetings,[11] and markets[12] are public events but are less marked by inter-group competition. However, they draw throngs of people from a wide area, and everyone is, in a sense, on display. It is especially young men and girls who like to dress up for markets. There is always the chance of impressing the crowd and meeting an old or making a new

Plate 27
Oiled and feathered,
men compete to finish a
section of road

Plate 28
Many of the road-workers
were painted with
charcoal and white clay

Plate 29
Variation on the same
pattern (see Plate 28)

acquaintance. The girls put on their beads, bangles, cloth, talcum powder, shells and flowers as usual, but probably not paint (Pl. 31); the men have neat cassowary, cockatoo, eagle, or marsupial tail head-dresses.

In summary, we can say that on these informal occasions decorations are worn either to express group competition, or to make oneself sexually attrac-

46

tive,[13] or simply in recognition of a public event. These are precisely the reasons for self-decoration on formal occasions also. For informal affairs people have rather more choice about whether to decorate themselves and how. Nevertheless, choice is not random. Many specific assemblages of items are reserved for the more formal *moka* and cult festivals, as we shall see.

Formal decorations are worn at festivals for ceremonial gifts of pigs and shells and at cult performances. In chapter one we have given some idea of the preparations for dancing at a festival. Here we must describe the rationale for the festivals and patterns of dancing at them.

The main types of exchange are those resulting from warfare in the past and those which we can designate as 'pure *moka*'.

The first type includes enemy-compensation and ally-reparation payments, which we can best describe with stereotyped examples. If group A killed a man of group B it may later compensate its enemies for the death, in order to restore good relations. This occurs only if the two groups are not major enemies. Again, if group A asked group B to help it as an ally against group C, and a man of B was killed, A should make reparations to B for this, or else face the loss of the alliance and also a possible threat of violence from B. Payments are made with both pigs and shells.

The second type (pure *moka*) also includes gifts of shells and pigs. In shell-*moka* sets of mounted pearl shells[14] are given away to exchange partners by the men of a donor group or a single big-man. Recipients receive the shells in sets of eight or ten, and for each set they privately (not on the occasion of the main festival) return a pig and two shells. The latter items can sometimes be looked on as soliciting the main gift. Pig-*moka* takes a similar form: sets of pigs are given away in return for smaller 'solicitory' gifts of pigs. An alternative is to kill pigs and present their meat to exchange partners.

In practice pure *moka* and warfare exchanges become intertwined. An important feature of all ceremonial exchange relations in Hagen is that they are expected to continue over a number of years. If one group compensates, reparates, or gives *moka* to another it expects that the recipients will reciprocate after a few years. *Moka* relations are explicitly based on this norm of reciprocity; war payments come to follow the same pattern since it is often the case that there have been reciprocal killings or reciprocal ally-losses between clans. Thus A pays B for losses and later B pays A, much as is done in *moka* itself.

War payments are also supposed to follow a sequence, starting from the time when a killing or loss has newly occurred. They begin with gifts of cooked pig, pass through presentations of pearl shells, and end with live pigs. Through a number of years they become converted into forms which resemble *moka* more and more closely. When the stage of exchanging live pigs is reached, participants say, 'Now we are making a road of *moka* between us.'

Moreover, there is a further factor involved in the relations between exchanging groups, which is important for us here: where groups are in reciprocal exchange relations they are likely to have been both allies and enemies to each ther on different occasions in the past. They are rivals, and in their exchanges they try to outdo each other by the total size of their gifts. Rivalry is built into the *moka* transaction as a premise, since the main gift should exceed the solicitory gifts in value and should also exceed previous *moka* gifts given by those now receiving. We are dealing with groups which confront and test each other over time with demonstrations of their wealth.

The style of dancing adopted seems to fit this accent on rivalry. It is very simple in movement, but effectively shows off the numbers of men and their decorations. Men don feathers, shells, leaves and grasses, face-paint and charcoal, and their best wigs, belts, and aprons. If women and girls are dancing formally, they are decked out with a profusion of items of the same general kind as those worn by the men, with long sweeping reed aprons, although they do not charcoal their faces or carry weapons. Girls and younger women who come as spectators are dressed in second-best attire, but their faces will almost certainly be painted.

There are two main dances for men, *mør* and *kanan*. Married women decorate themselves and dance formally only for pig-moka, and then not always, but only if the display is to be a large one. For such an occasion their dance is called *werl*; at other times they, or more particularly unmarried girls, perform *mørli*, quite different in character, which requires little more decoration than is worn for courting parties.

In *mør*, male dancers form in a single line (Pl. 32, Col. pl. 6) or extend into a

Plate 32
Holding drums, dancers line up for *mør* (Northern Melpa)

horseshoe round the ceremonial ground with donors and recipients facing each other. Drum and whistle notes may punctuate the dancing. With a sharp, opening yodel, all begin to sing. The dance consists of a stately, rhythmic genuflection, the drums beaten just as the legs are straightened and the body reaches an upward crescendo. After a few minutes a faster rhythm is adopted, involving constant pivoting on the toes. Then there is a rest, till someone starts singing or drumming again. Those without drums hold spears, which, lifting up and down in unison, they point at the spectators. As the men move, their plumes sway backwards and forwards, and light catches on the feathers and on their shell ornaments, while the long aprons billow out in front.

For *kanan*[15] men form into ranks, consisting of rows of four or more across, and stamp round the ceremonial ground in time with each other. They maintain rows by locking arms or by holding a spear horizontally in front of them (Pl. 33). Or they may space out further from each other and grasp bow and arrows in the left hand, an axe in the right. *Kanan* is favoured for impressive group entrances (Col. pl. 4), or to wind up a session of *mør*; or it can be performed on its own.

In both types of dance the men concentrate on their posture, staring out unseeingly at the crowd of jostling spectators. Their decorations, they say, help them by making them harder to recognise as individuals. This point seems surprising, in view of the stress which is also laid on individual rivalry between the dancers. One can resolve the paradox, perhaps, by suggesting that men do not aim at making it *impossible* to recognise them, but only at making it difficult, so that recognition comes with some surprise. It is also the case that as clansmen they can recognise and appraise each other easily enough under their 'disguise'; while outsiders who do not know them well will simply evaluate their performance as a whole group. The individual rivalry is internal to the group of dancers themselves.

At festivals where pigs are actually killed and cooked for distribution, another dance, *ware*, may traditionally be performed. Dancing then takes place for three days before the pigs are slaughtered, and on the fourth men take off their decorations and work at preparing the meat. Each man distributes meat to his individual exchange partners. Decorations for *ware* and a similar dance called simply 'cooked pig dance' (*kng kui*) sometimes resemble those of non-Melpa-speaking Wahgi Valley people. (At smaller pig-kills, for which a block gift of pig-meat is handed over by one group to another, there may be no dancing at all, and if so there is correspondingly less emphasis on decorations.)

Married women do not dance in the *mør* and *kanan* sequences, but a few unmarried girls occasionally join the *mør*. Either they enter the line spontaneously, as a mark of favour for a particular dancer, or they take part on a

Plate 33
Kanan formation
(Nebilyer Valley)

formal basis and their decorations closely parallel those of their male clanmates, except in their face-paint, wigs, and aprons. In the latter case they are on display for potential husbands to see. If a man has no sons, his eldest unmarried daughter can also dance in the *kanan* (but does not hold weapons, which are exclusive to men)[16] (Pl. 69).

Married women, as we have mentioned, dance in elaborate decorations only for pig-*moka*, and they do so specifically to celebrate their success in rearing pigs which their husbands are giving away to exchange partners. Shell payments are exclusively men's affairs; but when men achieve renown by the size of their *moka* pigs, they are expected to recognise the wives' contribution by making them glamorous for a day. Men say that women dirty themselves in muddy paths and gardens and bear the brunt of food-getting and pig-rearing; and that hence their husbands are sorry for them and help them gather decorations for the final *moka* dance.[17]

For a pig-*moka* dance, then, while men line up for *mør* or stamp round in *kanan* formation, heavily decorated women appear one by one at the edge of the ceremonial ground. Each holds a drum (little daughters may be decorated, too, but do not always have drums [Col. pl. 18]). The women dance *werl*, which consists of a measured bowing from side to side, in time with drum-beats and singing. Gradually they swing more in one direction, until they turn right round and display their backs to spectators (mainly other women and girls). Their backs are profusely decorated with shells and leaves, to an extent greater than in the case of men (Pl. 34). Whereas women ornament their whole bodies with equal elaborateness, the emphasis for men tends to be on the head. We shall return later to the significance of head decorations for Hageners.

The men complete the day by charging aggressively up and down the ceremonial ground where pigs are tethered to stakes, weapons in hand, and by making formal speeches in a special chanting style, ending each phrase with a long‑drawn‑out oh – oh – oh.[18] They explain the reasons for the gift, announce further plans and boast of their prowess. The wives of the donors, who have been dancing *werl*, move more slowly up and down the row of pigs, beating their drums, as a sign that it is really they who have enabled the *moka* to take place. Finally, one of the donors walks down the row and gives each pig a ceremonial kick, saying, 'Kill this and cook it!', as an act of completing the transfer.

At other types of exchange festival women and girls dance only the *mørli*, for which they wear much less decoration, as it is peripheral to the main business of display by men. In *mørli* the dancers gather intimately in one or more circles, linking arms, and enclose other females as spectators. One of them leads a chanting song, and as this reaches a shrieking crescendo they jump up and down lustily, and the circle moves round (Pl. 35). *Mørli* is thus a dance carried out with high spirits, in which young women draw attention to them‑selves; it is, in fact, a kind of group invitation to young men to turn‑head when the main transactions are over. The songs are really courting songs, whereas women dancing *werl*, like the men executing *mør* or *kanan*, sing refrains which have political themes – commenting on the display of strength and wealth, throwing taunts at rivals or enemies. *Mørli* is to do with sex; *werl* is concerned with the serious world of pigs and exchange.

For *mørli* girls paint their faces in triangles, stipples, and streaks, of blue, yellow, and red, with eyes ringed in white (Col. pl. 26). They remove their net‑bags but may retain a bright red trade‑cloth over their backs. They may wear a cassowary quill through the septum, for this is thought to be sexually alluring. They have oiled their bodies and perhaps put crinkled red cordylines over their aprons. The aprons themselves they tie between the legs, giving a kind of horse‑tail appearance, by which means they preserve a little modesty while they dance. They have no feathers, and few shells or furs; and the absence of these decoration items indicates how peripheral they are to the main business of the day. Married women who join in may not be decorated at all.

While men are dancing or speech‑making they appear to ignore the *mørli*, except for occasionally shouting to the girls to be less noisy or to move away.

Plate 34
The lavish decorations of women dancing *werl*

Plate 35
A *mørli* circle

Meanwhile the *mørli* circle grows in size. When important matters are over, the younger and more energetic men doff their tall plumes and begin a rival dance called *yap*.[19] Their circle swells till it dominates the ceremonial ground; they move round fast and continuously, without the ecstatic shrieks and jumps of the girls. Songs usually become ribald, and dialogue develops through them between the rival circles of men and girls. Young men may now even join the women's circle, perhaps to dance with a turning-head partner.

Mørli episodes, although they are aside from the actual exchanges of wealth at a *moka*, do relate clearly to one of the aims of self-decoration, that is to make oneself sexually attractive. A sequence of exchange festivals, in fact, triggers off courting parties; after a day's dancing young men frequently spend the night turning-head; and during the formal dance itself, as we have mentioned, girls may break into the line of men and link arms with a dancer they admire, jogging up and down with him. This is a mark of favour and it brings some prestige to the man chosen (Pl. 75).

At a deeper level, attracting the opposite sex is thought of as cognate with the ability to attract wealth to oneself. That is why dancers have to be not only impressive but also 'attractive'.

There is one other context in which women play a part at *moka* dances: this is called the display of 'women with netbags full of greens'.[20] It is performed only occasionally, when a particular 'message' is to be relayed to spectators. For it, women are deliberately dressed in a reversal of what would constitute good decorations. They wear no feathers, begrime their faces and bodies with charcoal, making themselves 'dark', and may even smear their heads with earth. They fill netbags with scraps of greens, nuts, and pig-tusks, and march silently, with heads down, around the men doing *mør*. The message involved in these decorations is a part of inter-clan politics and is an aggressive one. If a clan related to the donors at the festival has been taunted for not making *moka*, its men may decorate some of their wives and sisters in this way and send them to the dance. The decorations are meant to say: 'All right, you our critics claim that we are "rubbish men". You whisper this behind our backs but we have heard it and so send our women along in rubbishy decorations, carrying nuts instead of shells, tusks instead of real pigs, scraps instead of true food. But later we shall show you this is just a pretence. We have good ground, excellent food, plenty of wealth, and we shall make *moka* and eclipse your prestige – so look out!'

This example reminds us that exchange festivals are meant to be demonstrations of strength and prosperity on the part of the donor clan. The political commentary of dancers' songs can be overtly hostile towards other groups.

Religious cults are similar demonstrations, but in addition their explicit aim is to promote prosperity and fertility by ritual action. Currently the two main cults practised in Hagen are the Female and Male Spirit cults (*Amb Kor* and *Kor Wøp*).[21]

Performances of these cults circulate from group to group, but any single clan group holds one only at intervals of many years. The chief cult objects are decorated stones (see Appendix II). These are in fact water-worn river stones or else prehistoric mortars and pestles of the kind which are commonly enough found throughout the New Guinea Highlands.[22] Men discover these stones while digging garden ditches or walking by rivers, or they inherit custodianship of them from their fathers. They keep them buried inside an enclosure marked by trees, at the back of a ceremonial ground. The Spirit connected with the stones shows its power by sending sickness to the clansmen who own them. Ritual experts diagnose the situation and prescribe a cult performance to satisfy and control the Spirit and to ensure future health. A sequence of sacrifices takes place within the enclosure, which is shut off by a number of high cane fences. The experts officiate, and see to the building of houses for the rituals and the digging of earth ovens. After what is often years of specific preparations, there is a final sacrificial cooking in the enclosure, the participants decorate themselves and dance, viewed by hundreds of spectators, many of whom receive gifts of pork.

The decorations worn for these cults are essentially similar in scale and magnificence to those worn for *moka* exchanges and war payments. They are similar also in style. But the cults have additional stylistic elements of their own, and we go into the details of these in the following chapter. We end this chapter by briefly discussing the meaning of the cult rituals themselves.

The Female Spirit cult is concerned both with fertility and with male purification. The Spirit is said to appear to men in dreams as a beautifully adorned young bride. Although she appears as a bride, she does not stay to bear children, but remains a virgin. It is perhaps this combination of femininity and purity that makes her an appropriate object for a cult which includes a ritual to protect men against the threat of menstrual pollution from their actual human wives. Protection is obtained by eating, within the cult enclosure, a ritual meal of forest herbs mixed with pig's kidneys. The theme of general fertility appears in another ritual sequence, in which pig-suet is taken and placed in a trench within the house where the cult stones are displayed; here the suet is described as 'grease' which helps to fertilise the earth. The ritual experts accompany every action with a spell. Most of the pig-meat is cooked in a long oven, covered with forest moss, which runs the length of one of the cult houses. This meat the performers then distribute, partly to the experts in payment for their services, and later partly to male exchange partners outside the enclosure. Women are in theory not supposed to eat this meat;

nor should they enter even the first part of the cult enclosure.[23] Although the cult centres on a Female Spirit it is emphatically an affair of the men (Pl. 36).

In the inner part of the enclosure men practise their Spirit-dance. They line up in pairs, each man holding a twist of ferns before him in place of the pearl shells he will later hold, and, with a quick shuffle-cum-stamp of the feet, move in a train round the cult house (Pl. 37). On the final day they decorate them-selves fully in secret, dance out of the cult place, and stream round the ceremonial ground (Pl. 38). As they flash out of the enclosure door, displaying their shells and waving their white plumes, the crowd shouts, 'The Spirit is coming!' They circle three times, then re-enter the enclosure, remove their feathers, and reappear on high platforms at the sides of the ceremonial area to distribute strips of pork among the upturned spears of visitors. This distribution over, the crowd rapidly disperses.

The *Wɵp* cult centres on actions designed to ensure clan strength and fertility. Like the Female Spirit cult, it can be performed only by men, but it stresses

Plate 36
Men open up a subsidiary cooking pit in the cult enclosure

56

relations between the sexes rather than male purification from the polluting power of women.

Some months before the final performance, ritual experts sacrifice pigs, take examples of the cult stones which resemble pestles and place them in mortars as a symbol of sexual intercourse; they wrap all the stones in moss saturated with pig's blood and bury them underneath a tall 'pole-house' with open sides and a bark roof, inside the cult enclosure. At the same time they divide out pig's liver to the initiates. Both of these ritual actions are to produce fertility and health.

Near by in the enclosure is a spring of water, called the 'Spirit's eye', which is regarded as a source of the same virtues. In front of the main sacrifice-pit there is a stake which represents the group of male participants themselves, and their penises are supposed to be made by the cult actions as erect as the stake itself is. The experts also plant a garden of tall sugar-cane and taro. Each small subgroup involved in the cult performance brings plants for this garden, which is set up at night-time. Next morning it is torn down and the pieces are thrown

Plate 37
In cassowary plumes, performers practise their dance

Plate 38
'The Spirit is coming!'

into the spring, with a libation of tree-oil. This is an offering of food and grease to the earth, again for fertility, which is reminiscent of the action of burying suet in the Female cult. Finally, the performers place their feather head-dresses inside the tall pole-house, where spirits of clan ancestors are supposed to cluster, to make the plumes bright before they don them and dance out.

The stress on fertility and sexuality shown in this cult seems consistent with the fact that women may take part in the climactic dance for it. They should strictly keep to the outer part of the enclosure (away from the chief ritual objects), and then precede the men out into the ceremonial ground over the main fence, which is hacked down at this time. (At a performance in 1965[24] the women actually marched right through to the inner enclosure, to the disgust of the ritual experts.) Two or three men, beating drums and weaving from side to side, accompany women, who trot and stamp in time (Pl. 65), then once they are outside fall into the *werl* dance, as for an exchange festival. Behind them comes

58

a solid mass of men, in rows of perhaps six across, thumping out an orthodox *kanan* or a more lively version, proper to the cult, called *poke* (Pl. 41). After making a procession about the ceremonial ground the men settle to a *mør* dance, continuing till the afternoon.

Both of these cults, then, end with massive public displays just as the exchange festivals do. Indeed they may be preceded by actual *moka* transactions and followed by distributions of meat. Rituals performed within the enclosures are inward-looking, designed to promote group well-being. The final dance, when the enclosure fence has been broken down, is a display by the group to show that they have achieved the cult aims. In the Female Spirit cult only men perform; but in the *Wøp* men and women dance together.

In this account of situations in which decorations are worn we have pointed to a general theme. The act of decorating is symbolic: it is a gesture of self-display, and what is being displayed is a person in an enhanced or ideal state. On formal occasions the dancers assert group prosperity and health; when people dress up informally they assert their personal well-being. This is the general 'message' which decorations convey, and in a very real sense they are both the medium in which the message is communicated and the message itself. An examination of the details of decoration will show us, further, that a whole battery of messages can be transmitted through different combinations of items.

Plate 39 Light charcoaling suits an 'Enga wig' made in readiness for a festival

CHAPTER FOUR

Decoration sets

In this chapter we look more closely at the decorations appropriate to different formal occasions. It is particularly types of feathers that distinguish between different festivals and different categories of dancers taking part in a single festival.

In considering decoration sets, as we call them, we shall also be dealing with aspects of colour symbolism; and one dimension of such symbolism emerges if we compare decorations worn for exchange and cult festivals with those put on for warfare. We leave detailed analysis of colour connotations until chapter seven, but provide in this chapter some of the basic material for later discussion. We should note that although the concept of a set of decorations appropriate for some occasion is seen in terms of items which go together, with very few exceptions[1] there are no verbal usages which refer to sets as wholes. One can say 'he is dressed to dance *mør*', but neither the feathers nor the total combination of plumes, apron, wig, and so on, are regularly named as discrete costumes. Hageners do not speak of decorations as comprising complete, standardised outfits, but as being composed of an assembled medley of elements, only some of which are diagnostic of a particular occasion or dance; and within the medley there is room for individual variation.

STANDARDISATION OF SETS

In informal decoration an individual is free to choose what exact combination of ornaments he decides to wear. He is nevertheless circumscribed by the general cultural consensus on what scale of decoration is suitable for particular functions. Since people dress up in order to be admired, it is in their interests to conform to general canons of taste. In the case of formal decorations constraints operate to a greater degree, for dances are attended by spectators, who actively criticise ill-assembled costumes. An individual lacking most of the major elements required for a dance would be put to shame by his failure to find the right decorations and would hesitate to take part at all.

We are dealing with two separate influences on decision-making here. There is first the cultural code, which defines what decorations it is appropriate to wear once all the social features of a festival have been agreed upon. Second, there is the actual process of deciding what festivals to hold and what dances to perform at them. The big-men are very important as promoters and pro-nouncers here. Once the dance has been decided on there may be few major variations possible in the decorations to be displayed. If *mør* is to be performed, this more or less entails a specific set of decorations, although the degree of social distance between the donors and recipients makes for further complica-tions, as we shall see. For *kanan* there is a choice of costume styles, and a public decision has to be made. Further variations depend on the roles of the partici-pants – whether they are the main donors, helpers, or recipients: what the reci-pients wear will follow from their knowledge of how the donors will be decorated. The final assemblages will thus result from an interplay of several fac-tors. At some points explicit decisions will be made, via suggestions of the big-men; at others the participants will know from the context what is required, provided the main agreement has already been publicised as to the type of ex-change and the dance to be carried out. When these features have been settled, there is little place for the individual to show innovation in his choice of the main elements.[2] Here we are treating wigs, feathers, and aprons[3] as the major diagnostic items for decoration sets. This requires a little further explanation.

If one asks a Hagener how he once decorated himself for a festival or what decorations suit a particular occasion, he replies with a list which includes both items which we have called 'main' and those we call 'accessories'.[4] But if one asks which items distinguish one festival or dance from another, he will select only 'main' items for mention. These basic components exert a certain amount of constraint on the choice of accessories also, and the constraints here are related to the overall effect aimed at in the decoration: for example, very bright face designs would not be suitable for wearing in combination with *køi wal* head-dresses, since these are meant to produce a relatively dark total impression. Face-paint, in fact, is so important to the total effect of decorations that perhaps it should be regarded as a main rather than an accessory item. We do not wish to make a rigid distinction here; to the Hagener, as we have said,

all the ornaments he wears for an occasion play a part in creating a total impression. But we also follow the Hageners in singling out wigs, feathers, and aprons
as main articles of dress. Face-paint gains its significance, we would suggest,
from the fact that it contributes to the decoration of the head, and to the colour
effect of the whole assemblage. It is closely linked to the symbolism of decorations.

Further items can more definitely be described as accessories, either because
they are not essential to an occasion, or because they receive less emphasis in
accounts given by the people themselves. Nevertheless, they, too, are all displayed for effect. On the one hand, men can differentiate themselves from each
other through the choice of these accessories (pendants, necklaces, furs, leaves,
and grasses); on the other hand, they should not wear items which are thoroughly
inappropriate to the occasion. Matters like this are tacitly understood (although
some individuals have a more subtle appreciation of them than others), and
they give rise to critical appraisal rather than dogmatic commands from the
big-men. Whether a dancer feels he has acquired enough suitable items to
approximate to the right costume is a matter for himself to decide. In some
circumstances he can dance with an incomplete complement. It may not, for
example, be necessary or even correct for everyone to wear the same set as the
leading performers. In addition, there are numerous variations in styles of
feather arrangements adopted by different groups at a given time; each may
change its styles over time, for there is an interchange of styles between groups;
and there are also overall changes in fashion which are common to a number of
groups – for instance, the older German literature on Hagen shows some
items which are not worn nowadays.[5]

SETS WORN FOR EXCHANGE FESTIVALS

Hageners distinguish exchanges between closely linked clans, often of the same
tribe, from occasions, typically larger ones, involving groups which are socially
more distant from, or politically more opposed to, each other. They describe
the former as 'internal exchange', the latter as 'sending the exchange gifts outside'. For internal exchange, donors need not wear the køi wal or King of Saxony
sprays. Consequently internal exchange need not be accompanied by a preliminary pig-cooking, since these cookings are especially associated, as we have
seen in chapter two, with giving payment for Saxony feathers brought by
kinsmen and friends for dancers to wear.

Saxony feathers, in fact, are reserved for the more important occasions.
When men are ready to make a big *moka*, they say, 'the bird is on its way',
meaning, 'now the Saxony plumes will appear'. The køi wal themselves include
these feathers.

The appropriate wig to wear with *køi wal* is nowadays the large horned one called *Enga peng* ('Enga wig')[6] which appears to be derived from the styles of the Enga people west of Hagen (see chapter one) (Pl. 39). These are not covered with a head-net as ordinary wigs are, and they present a striking, dark appearance, which fits the blue plumage in the *køi wal* and the dark effect of charcoaled faces.[7] Little yellow feathers[8] or nowadays twirled pieces of cotton-wool are used to pick out the wig's black edges (Col. pl. 8).

These wigs are often constructed on a base of burrs. Helpers shape clusters of burrs on a piece of bark-cloth placed over the future wearer's head. When a satisfactory shape is achieved, it is covered with human hair. Before a big *moka* all the men of a clan are busy helping each other to make wigs, and they often refer to their progress in speeches.

The wig's large, flat, sunken top provides a good support for the *køi wal* head-dresses (Col. pl. 7). Previously men constructed the *wal* by attaching plu-mage to a trellis of bamboo sticks (Pl. 40) backed with pandanus leaves, but now the pandanus is usually replaced by cardboard or thick paper.[9] Saxony feathers, doubled and placed vertically, divide the backing into three areas; the two out-side portions are dark blue, and the centre is red with insets of bright blue, green, or yellow – all made from tiny parrot feathers stitched together. The insets form squares, triangles, or diamonds (the latter called *nomong*, the same term as is used for diamond designs painted on the cheek; cf. chapter five)[10] (Pls 45, 46). At the top is a fringe of lorikeet feathers or fluff from the white breast of an eagle. The King of Saxony plumes are described as running down the assem-blage like streams of water.[11] Flanking them on the outside edges there may be Sicklebill feathers. The whole is set on a pair of bamboo slivers for attachment to the wig.

At either side of the *køi wal* men wear feathers of the Blue bird. The delicate plumes are bound to a slender stick about a foot long (Col. pls 9, 10). (Nowa-days coarse blue wool may substitute for feathers, since the Blue bird is appa-rently becoming rarer;[12] but the substitute is regarded as inferior, and is worn only if a man cannot obtain the original.) Behind the *wal* and waving above it there should be a single plume or more of the Red bird, again set on a support to give it height. And at a still greater height men may wear a further Saxony spray. To a long cassowary quill they attach a nut kernel filled with sticky gum (Pl. 45). Mounted on this structure, the feathers can sway back and forth in time to the graceful genuflection of the *mør* dance: a movement which the Hageners connect with the gleam of the feathers as light catches them (Col. pl. 16).

Usually worn with this head-dress are long dance aprons (*mbal omb*), which reach nearly to the ground and repeat the swaying motion of the plumes as the

Plate 40
A Saxony plume is
adjusted

dancers move (Pl. 41). These aprons are finely netted, and decorated with stripes dyed in dark blue alternating with interwoven marsupial fur. A man can make do with a rather irregular combination of feathers, but he would never dance without a proper apron. They are regarded as dark, and are considered to fit the *køi wal* in particular.

It is this particular set of feathers – *køi wal*, Blue bird, Red plume at the back and Saxony sprays above – that marks out the group of the donors at important exchange festivals (e.g. Col. pl. 6). The recipients, and men of other allied clans who come to help the donors by dancing, do not normally wear *køi wal*, but instead appear with an assortment of Red, Blue, and other feathers which is rather similar to those worn for internal exchanges (e.g. Col. pl. 14).

At internal exchanges there is not such a sharp distinction made between donors and other dancers. Feathers worn by donors, helpers and recipients alike are eagle, *kumin* (we use the Melpa term since the identification of this with Palm cockatoo (Table 1) is only tentative),[14] Blue, Red, and the dark velvet

Plate 41
Big-men leading a *kanan* formation wear Saxony sprays (Nebilyer Valley, *Wøp* cult)

Plate 42
Donors at the Ndika festival in *køi wal* and 'Enga wigs'

ruff of the Lesser Superb bird (Col. pl. 12). The donors, however, tend to have a fuller complement of feathers. If eagle or *kumin* plumes are chosen, it is unlikely that the Blue will be worn as well, for the former are massed in large numbers which cover the wig and leave little room for other types (Pl. 43).

As we have mentioned, face-paint styles depend on the wig and feathers adopted and thus on the kind of occasion which is being celebrated. For important festivals when *køi wal* are worn, the donors should blacken their faces heavily with charcoal, while picking out the eyes (or nose, mouth, or cheeks) in stripes or stipples of white. The nose may be partly coloured red. These small areas of white or red colour contrast with, but at the same time highlight, the overall dark appearance of the faces (Col. pl. 9). It is the same here as for the rest of the donor's decorations: *køi wal*, Enga wig and dyed aprons are all said to be predominantly dark, although the effect is deliberately relieved by white shells and bright furs and plumes[15] (cf. Col. pl. 10). For recipients and helpers brighter colours are allowed. At the smaller festivals (internal exchanges) all categories of male dancers can have brighter colouring. We may generalise that, while on every occasion the dancer is an amalgam of bright and dark decorations, for the more important events 'darkness' is emphasised.

Plate 43
A helper wears eagle feathers and striped knitted head-net

Plate 44
Young Ndika helper

68

We should underline again that it is largely the head decorations which carry the marks that distinguish sets from each other. Weapons, drums, shells, furs, arm and belt bands, beads, leaves, and grasses may not vary at all between the different categories of dancers. The effect is to lay emphasis on the head rather than other parts of the body.

So far we have noted distinctions between donors, helpers, and recipients. A further complication is that recipients also may call in helpers of their own. Helpers are either men of a linked sub-clan within the clan of the donors or recipients, or men of linked clans in a tribe, or of an extra-tribal ally clan. The helpers may be planning to make *moka* themselves and use the occasion of helping others partly as a practice dance for themselves.

We have remarked that helpers of the donors' group are usually distinguished from the men of the actual donor clan. If they are planning a *moka* they may have already made their Enga wigs. Otherwise they wear ordinary head-nets with insets of marsupial fur, and feathers as we have already described. However, if a small tribe wishes to assert its unity in display before an enemy tribe, its men may all dance together and wear *køi wal*, even though only one of its clans is the donor group and the others are simply its helpers. Other helpers, from outside the tribe, would not wear *køi wal* in this way. The recipients and their helpers never put it on, unless they wish to indicate that they, too, will be donors in another *moka* soon; and then only a few big-men among them would take it upon themselves to display the *wal* or Saxony sprays, their action here indicating both their general high status and the prominent part they take in decisions about when to hold *moka* festivals. In such cases donors and recipients are still differentiated, for among the former it is a matter of importance that as many as possible should wear the *wal* and Saxony feathers, whereas among the latter only a few will do so, and this is by their private decision, while the donors must come to a group consensus about their dress.

Occasionally big-men may even make outrageous choices of what to wear, perhaps just to differentiate themselves from others: as when one big-man wore a large Enga wig, sticks of wool instead of Blue feathers, and left part of his face unpainted, for an occasion when nearly everyone else wore ordinary round head-nets and eagle feathers, and painted their faces fully in black and white. He was, paradoxically, short of ornaments at the time, and had been unsuccessful in last-minute attempts at borrowing; but, unlike an unimportant man, he did not allow this to deter him from taking part in the dance.[16] He knew that his status and the fact that his oratorical abilities were needed for the later speech-making would easily carry him through (Pl. 48).

Big-men sometimes wear Saxony sprays even when they are not donors but recipients at a *moka*. These sprays are, in fact, a mark of some eminence in

Plate 45
Judging the effect of a
newly assembled *koi wal*

Plate 46
Men from the same settlement area display their *køi wal* before a dance

the exchange system (Pl. 41), and they are not universally worn by donors either, even if the donor group is wearing *køi wal*. One reason is that the Saxony feathers are fairly rare and not all men can afford to pay for borrowing them as well as the standard *køi wal*. The wearing of these plumes by big-men accentuates their status; when they are worn by recipient big-men the act also indicates an anticipation of their later role as chief donors when the direction of the *moka* gifts is reversed.

EXCHANGE FESTIVALS OBSERVED

We have so far given an outline of two sets of decorations which dancers are expected to wear at exchange festivals. Details on some of the dances we observed between 1964 and 1967 will help to show how far these expectations are in practice realised.

We take first a dance held in the Nebilyer Valley by Temboka speakers. In 1967 a sub-clan of Ndika tribe danced to celebrate an occasion at which its men (a) paid a reparation gift of pearl shells to allies; (b) gave pearl shells to some extra-clan kinsmen who had taken refuge with them and since returned home; and (c) gave away some pigs in *moka*.

All the recipients were of tribes different from that of the donors. Moreover, the chief recipients were the allies, the other two gifts being subsidiary ones. Hence there was a considerable note of rivalry in the occasion. One big-man among the donors boasted of his small group's strength in giving as many as 400 shells to its allies. (Further, at least one man from the group's actual enemies attended the event, and the same speaker directed a fiery tirade against him.) The occasion was thus treated by the donors as an important one, even though the numbers of men dancing were remarkably small (thirty in all). It is consistent with this that they nearly all wore *køi wal*, with Red, Saxony, and Blue plumes as well (Pl. 42, Col. pl. 6). One or two who lacked the *wal* made up their head-dresses with larger and more numerous Red plumes (Col. pls 13, 15). Some men added fluffy white cockatoo or eagle breast feathers as optional accessories to the rims of their Enga wigs – this would be a matter of private decision. In Appendix III we show the range of individual variation in head-dresses among the dancers.

The donors' helpers came from a linked sub-clan of their own clan, but despite their close relationship they had decided to wear quite distinct decora-tions from the donors themselves: round, knitted head-nets (Pl. 43) in contrast with many of the donors' angular Enga wigs, and an assortment of Red, eagle, *kumin*, turkey, or peacock[17] plumes instead of *køi wal* (Pls 44, 47).

Why was this distinction made between the decorations, although donors and their helpers were of the same clan? In terms of the cultural code such a

Plate 47
Dressing: eagle (L) and *kumin* (R) feather head-dresses

distinction should imply a social distance between the two categories of dancers rather greater than usually exists between sub-clans of a clan. In this case, however, the social distance between the two *had* recently increased. The helpers, perhaps urged on by their own big-men, had given *moka* earlier to one of the recipient groups, and this in itself was contrary to the expectation that linked sub-clans should stage their *moka* at the same time. We do not know the specific political background to this occasion, but it is a general feature of Hagen clans (as of all societies marked by segmentary political relations) that there is both cohesion and opposition between their segments. We can safely say that the two sub-clans here were rivals and that their big-men are likely to have been leading instigators of this rivalry. The unity of the sub-clans was thus already shaken by their *moka* disagreement: in a sense, the helpers had put the donors to shame by completing their own *moka* in advance; and the increased antagonism between them was reflected in their differing decorations. In fact, the occasion made it possible for this antagonism to be expressed; if the helpers had not danced at all, they could not have acted out their feelings so effectively. As it was, they made a separate entrance to the ceremonial ground, doing *kanan*, and stamped right past the donors before taking up stations at the far end of their line.

Another feature of this occasion was that the recipients did not dance. Here the reason seems to have been that they were busy preparing for a *moka* of their own but had not yet gathered their decorations. Some of them, including their leader, came wearing brown cassowary head-dresses, which in this context signified that their *moka* was impending.

Compare the patterns here with those in a *moka* held among the Northern Melpa in 1964. This was a preliminary to a larger occasion which took place six months later. A pair of clans of the Kawelka tribe were due to receive ally-reparation payments from a similar pair among their eastern neighbours, the Tipuka tribe. At this preliminary event the Kawelka presented their Tipuka allies with a large solicitory gift of pigs.

For this occasion the Kawelka did not wear *køi wal*, but Red plumes, Saxony sprays, and eagle or *kumin* feathers. These last two types were not planted in a circlet round the wigs as is done in Temboka, but mounted according to local custom on a length of softwood worn above the wig itself (Pl. 48). Several men also wore Blue bird plumes and the breast shield and cape plumage of the Superb bird.

Not every man had exactly the same combination of these feathers. The main combinations (excluding Saxony sprays, on which our data are not precise) were: (1) Red+(eagle or *kumin*); (2) Red+(eagle or *kumin*)+(Blue and/or Superb); (3) Red+(Blue and/or Superb). (1) and (2) were about equally common; (3) much less so, probably because eagle and *kumin* feathers help to

Plate 48
Kawelka dance *mør* in eagle, *kumin* and Red bird feathers

fill the wigs with plumes and are popular for this reason. A few donors wore Enga wigs, which they had made in anticipation of the later occasion, but the tone of the dance was set by the majority who wore the ordinary knitted head-net.

Some 70 men and 12 boys danced as members of the donors' groups. The helpers (of the third clan in the donor's tribe) and the recipients, who together amounted to 55 men, wore basically the same assemblages as the donors.[18] Overall, however, their decorations were less ample: combination (3) was perhaps preponderant. Some wore Princess Stephanie tails instead of Red plumes.

By contrast with the previous occasion discussed, this event reveals little differentiation between the donors, helpers, and recipients, even though the gifts were 'sent outside' to allies of another tribe. The reason is that this was only a preliminary to the final *moka*, and the similarity of all the dancers' decorations fits the fact that their roles were not sharply differentiated. At the final *moka*, when the Tipuka became donors, over 300 men danced, and the Tipuka

74

distinguished themselves from the others by wearing *køi wal*, Enga wigs, and associated feathers as a set (Col. pl. 5). Large crowds turned up to watch, and the donors stampeded up the ceremonial ground to bring forward a capping gift of extra pigs. They were clearly displaying their strength in opposition to the recipients.

Our third example is a pig-*moka* given in 1967 by one sub-clan to two others of a different clan within the Kuli tribe. The Kuli we may call Eastern Melpa; they live near to the Wahgi Valley people of Minj and Banz. We choose this example partly because it gives us a case of women dancing in full decoration, and partly because the decorations themselves reflected the cultural influence on the Kuli of the Wahgi speakers.

The *moka* was an internal exchange, preliminary to a larger occasion at which the Kuli as a whole would be donors to an outside tribe. Yet it was marked by splendid decorations, Enga wigs, and *køi wal*. The explanation is that the dance was looked on as a practice for the larger event and a sign that the Kuli would soon be ready to make their big *moka*. They were hurrying to complete their preparations in advance of another tribe which was also nearing a climax of its *moka* activities. These factors help to explain the intensity of the display, why donors were mingled in the dancing formation with recipients and helpers, and why nearly all the men (not just the donors) wore the horned Enga wig. The dancing of the women was part of this general display too; but in particular the pigs given away were very large and each donor gave ten. It was to celebrate their individual success in rearing the pigs that the donors' wives decorated themselves. Other women joined them as helpers, wives of men who would soon be making *moka* and wives of recipients.

The event was called 'Princess Stephanie *moka*', from the fact that some of the men and women wore tails of the Princess Stephanie bird. Emphasis on this bird, and the similar Sicklebill tails (Pl. 49), reflected the influence of Banz and Minj styles; and our informants from other Melpa areas who saw the dance or photographs of it had difficulty in interpreting the 'code' by which donors and others were mutually distinguished. However, some distinctions were fairly clear.

Donors and their more closely related clansmen (helpers) wore *køi wal* with Saxony sprays (Col. pl. 4). The larger type of Sicklebill tails substituted for *køi wal* in some cases. Blue, Superb, and Red plumes, arranged in standard Melpa style, accompanied either of these arrangements. Other helpers and recipients wore Princess Stephanie and/or the shorter kind of Sicklebill tails (in contrast with the long ones of the donors), along with Red, White, and Blue plumes, or the same with numbers of spitted red and green lorikeets (Pl. 50). Helpers and recipients were a little more restrained in their decorations

75

Plate 49
Kuli dancers wearin
(L–R) Princess
Stephanie, Sicklebil
Red bird of paradise
plumes

Plate 50
Short Sicklebill feathers
(L) and a wig studded
with parrots and lorikeets
(R)

than the donors. For example, some wore only a single Red plume, set on a hoop above their wigs.

The married women dancers who performed *werl* contrasted with the men in the greater profusion of their ornaments and in their brighter face-paint (Col. pl. 19). Whereas the men wore only one or two Red plumes, women had as many as five, in a fan above their heads. Individual men wore perhaps three or four different kinds of plume, where women wore six to eight; and the overall number of birds represented in men's head-dresses we counted as twelve, the figure for women's being eighteen. The results in the relative appearance of the sexes were clear: while men's feathers were arranged discretely about their wigs, women's were crowded thickly; from circlets of bright red parrot feathers rose thick plantations of eagle or *kumin* faced with Superb shields; topping these were fans of Red plumes, and from these again rose the long black Sicklebill feathers which marked out wives of the actual donors (Pls 7, 51, Col. pl. 23).

This contrast between men and women was not the outcome of competition between them. Indeed women are dependent on their husbands and kinsmen to supply them with feathers. The women's decorations may well, however, have reflected minor rivalry between individual women themselves; and they clearly reflected the relative importance of the men who were donors on this occasion, since it was the donors' wives who were most elaborately decked out.

Women's faces were painted with blue and white (occasionally yellow) designs on a red base, whereas men's faces were charcoaled. The women also had long yellow aprons (made from sedge or lily plants),[19] and had fixed bright green, red, and yellow cordyline leaves at their waist and back. In addition to necklaces of cowries and swathes of beads, their breasts were covered with single shining white convex bailer shells.

Only one woman followed the custom of wearing a large mounted pearl shell at her back (Col. pl. 25, cf. Pl. 79). Such a shell is given by a woman's husband to her kinsfolk after the dance is over, in part recognition of their help in providing her with ornaments for the occasion. The shell is worn at the back because, men say, 'A wife's people are at her back, while she faces her husband.' The saying neatly comments on the fact that a woman leaves her kin (turns her back to them) when she marries and goes to her husband's place; and that she has a sexual relationship with her husband, whom she faces when she comes as a bride, while she retains kin ties with her natal group. (Ancestral ghosts are also said to be at people's backs, exercising an unseen influence over them; in the same way a woman's kin are expected to influence her.)

The full set of distinctions made among the women themselves demarcated the following categories: (a) donors' wives (Pl. 51); (b) wives of recipients and those of helpers among the Kuli who were due to make *moka* soon (Pls 52, 53); and (c) wives of Kuli men whose *moka* was planned for much later (Pl. 56). In addition, (d) young girls who accompanied their mothers received slightly different decorations (Pl. 54, also Pl. 10); (e) a few older girls danced *mør* with the men and wore ornaments different from those for *werl* (Pl. 55); and yet other girls (f) were only lightly decorated, and performed *mørli*.

Categories (a) and (b) were distinguished from each other in that the donors' wives, as we have said, wore the longer type of Sicklebill tail-feathers and also had a more profuse overall array. Otherwise they had the same range of ornaments as (b). Recipients' wives were distinguished to some extent from those of helpers, in that they had few eagle feathers. Women of category (c) were very clearly marked off from the other two, for they wore few feathers, at most a small circlet, although up to their foreheads they were adorned as much as the others.[20]

The girls in category (e) were dressed a little more like the men, with whom they were doing *mør*; for example, they had small topknots of feathers including

Plate 51
Donor's wife (Kuli),
her head-dress half
her own height

Plate 52
Recipient's wife with
parrot and multiple
bird of paradise plu▸

Plate 53
Dark *kumin* feathers set
off Red bird sprays,
trimmed with parrot

the Superb bird. One had a set of bamboo tally sticks which must have belonged to a male kinsman, and a thick string apron similar to those worn by women of Banz. The girls' faces, however, were brightly painted in white, red, and blue, and they wore crimped red cordylines over their aprons like the other women (Col. pl. 17).

This completes our description of decorations worn for three actual festivals. The examples show that the scale and elaboration of the ornaments depend partly on the relationship between donors and recipients, but also on whether the occasion is seen as a dress-rehearsal for a large, climactic festival. Further, the degree to which donors are differentiated from helpers and recipients depends on the way they conceive of their current political relations; at the Ndika *moka*, relations between the donors and their helpers were strained and this was reflected in their different head-dresses; whereas in the Kawelka and Kuli cases donors and helpers presented a more solidary front. In all instances, however, donors were distinguishable, either by some type of feather worn or, less

Plate 54
The decoration of a little girl

Plate 55
An unmarried girl dances *mør* with male kinsmen

82

aliently, by the profusion of their decorations; and this was true of the women as well.

We now look at a further range of decorations, in particular different types of head-dress and the occasions to which they are appropriate.

CASSOWARY FEATHERS

The Enga wig and *køi wal* can be worn for all exchange festivals and for both of the two main dances (*mør* and *kanan*). But there are certain other decorations which are restricted to special kinds of dances, festivals or stages in festivals. Two kinds of cassowary head-dress provide examples here.

The first is *køi kundil*, a cone of black cassowary feathers, stuck or bound to a frame, which is filled with burrs. A black-palm pin attaches it to the wig.[21] The *kundil* indicates that its wearer is giving away a set of ten shells and it is worn only for shell-moka. A big-man may himself wear a number, and give

33

others to his sons or place them on a spear. In the past, when each man put on his *kundil* a ritual expert spoke a spell, invoking birds of prey (which obtain meat, likened to valuables) and bower birds (which build dancing places like men's ceremonial grounds), as a means of drawing in more shells to his group.

The *kundil* was put on after men had finished dancing and had removed their full head-dresses. It was regarded as especially dark in its colour effect and its wearers blackened their bodies with charcoal to heighten this. Each donor in turn stood on the special mound which is raised around a tree [22] at one end of the ceremonial ground, handed over a set of shells, including one fine example to cap the gift, and at the same time doffed his *kundil*.[23]

The second special use of cassowary plumes is one we have already mentioned; they signify that their wearers will soon be making *moka*. At the Ndika *moka* described above the recipients marched in with blackened faces, holding weapons and wearing brown cassowary head-dresses (*køi kngal*) (Pl. 57). Their business-like air indicated that they were girding themselves to hold their own festival. The *kngal*, unlike the *kundil*, is regarded as 'bright' from its light brown colour.

What explains these usages? In part they are simply an extension of cassowary feathers as second-best wear. More specifically, they are 'liminal' usages, marking entry into or exit from the state of making *moka*. They come just before or just after full ceremonial head-dresses are worn.

It is also interesting to note here an emphasis on darkening oneself at the final stage of a festival, when the accent is on the actual gift rather than the dancing; when, that is, instead of displaying themselves to the general world of spectators, the donors specifically take up a stance, with a touch of rivalry and menace in it, towards the recipients. In later chapters we shall look more closely at the meaning of 'dark' and 'bright' categories relating to the overall effect of decora-tions; and we shall find that the same theme emerges from our discussion of special wig types and aprons to which we now turn.

SPECIAL WIGS AND APRONS

Heavy 'judge's wigs',[24] lined with scarab beetles and marsupial furs, and brightly painted with a variety of designs, are known throughout the Wahgi Valley[25] and to groups further east;[26] and a type of hair-setting which the Hageners make is also worn by the Maring in the Jimi and Simbai Valleys.[27] These are all areas neighbouring or almost neighbouring the Melpa speakers. We are not sure if the wigs are worn in Temboka, and their distribution in the Melpa area itself is uneven: they seem to have been most common among the Central Melpa. Some groups towards the Wahgi and in the Jimi specialised

Plate 57
A leading recipient: spear, stone axe, brown cassowary plume, and a wig he will later uncover at his own dance

5

in hair-setting. We do not know the history of the wigs' adoption by different groups (Pl. 58, Col. pl. 30).

Unlike other wigs, the 'judge's wig' forms a kind of canopy which completely surrounds the back of the head and may rest on the shoulders. Central Melpa speakers distinguish two kinds according to their length. *Peng koem*, 'the *koem* head', is the longer, falling right over the shoulders; *peng kuklnga*, 'the *kuklnga*-rope head', named after a liana used in making its frame, reaches to the shoulders only. The hair-setting is *peng kilt*, 'the *kilt*-resin head', so called from the tree resin which is used to set the hair.

Only men wore these head-dresses, and only a few men wore them at a given festival. They were made secretly in a special enclosure or in men's houses; and their makers were supposed not to have intercourse with their wives during this time, since, if they did so, it was thought that the head-dresses would be dull instead of bright and their own skins would become slack and dry.

This taboo on sexual contact with women parallels others which are supported by similar sanctions: for instance, the taboo on intercourse while wives are menstruating (such intercourse would not only harm men's skins but could result in sickness and death); on intercourse while men are making weapons (for the weapons would become weak and would break easily in battle); and on intercourse while men are preparing to decorate for a dance (for if they did so, the grease in their gourds, which they rub on their skins to make it bright, would dry up). All these rules imply that male strength and health can be jeopardised by contact with women, and it is especially when men wish to enhance their strength that they must avoid intercourse. The wigs and hair-setting, we suggest, are just such an enhancement of male strength, and it is significant that they form part of decorations for the head, which in the case of men receives most decorative emphasis in general.

We use the past tense for description of the manufacture of these head-dresses, as we have not seen the process ourselves. We do not wish to imply that the wigs have gone irrevocably out of fashion, but merely that most of the accounts we have relate to some years ago.[28]

Among the Central Melpa, *koem* and *kuklnga* were made, referred to, and worn in pairs, and called by one group[29] male and female wigs (perhaps to express the fact of their pairing and the larger size of the *koem*). Their wearers also danced in pairs.

To make *koem*, men first teased out rubbish and grease from the wearer-to-be's own hair-cuttings. They also cleaned hair collected from other men, wives and women of other groups (these last were paid for the service). Women's long ringlets were useful for the side-pieces, men's hair for the topknot. There seems to have been no incongruity perceived in the use of women's hair for a specifi-

Plate 58
Peng koem

cally male ornament.[30] Before beginning, men cooked a pig as a sacrifice to ancestral ghosts, who are especially associated with head-hair, to ensure that the wig would be bright.

The wig was built on a frame of pliant cane strips, bound with lianas. To this the manufacturers fastened lengths of hair, sewing them with a flying-fox bone needle and bark thread. They placed the completed wig on a stand underneath a banana stem which was slung horizontally across supports. Lumps of melted resin from the *kilt* tree (Rutaceae *Evodiella* and *Evodia* sps.) were placed on the banana stem and allowed to drip on to the wig in order to set the hair hard. The makers next smoothed the surface down with a rolling-pin, and rubbed pig or pandanus grease over it. Inside the frame they placed a

87

bark-cloth lining. Finally they painted the wig in bright colours with chevrons, streaks, triangles, or a design called after wings of the swiftlet (Col. pl. 30).[31] The term for most of these patterns are the same as those used to describe face-paint designs (which we detail later), and the pigments were added explicitly to brighten the wig which would otherwise remain dark from the colour of the hair.

On the day of dancing its wearer and his helpers would further fringe the wig with scarab beetles enclosed in bands of yellow orchid vine, light-coloured furs, and the leaves of a plant which is used in *moka* ritual to attract valuables. The topknot was left unpainted, but round it twined another bright fur, while from it sprang a medley of feathers set in a circlet. Red, White, and *kumin* feathers were considered suitable to wear, since the wig should not be topped with too many heavy plumes which might make it look dark. (The Northern Melpa wore Princess Stephanie and Sicklebill tails instead of *kumin*.)

Both in the painting of the wig and in the choice of feathers for its topknot, there was an explicit preference for a bright effect, which contrasts directly with the emphasis on a dark appearance for the *køi wal*. We shall argue that such aesthetic preferences are closely related to the symbolic meaning of these decorations.

Northern Melpa applied the term '*kuklnga* wig' not to the shorter version of *koem* as Central Melpa do, but to a hair-setting which is more like our third type, '*kilt* head'. For this setting, the growing hair of the man himself was teased into a dome and *kuklnga* rope (Euphorbiaceae *Claoxylon* sp.) interwoven with it to make it stiff. It was then anointed with tree-oil and resin and partly rolled into ringlets. The resin was kneaded right into the hair. Next, the makers took small, fluffy feathers from the eagle, Sulphur-crested cockatoo and red parrot, and fixed these to the hair. Over the sides of the setting they bound halves of long white *mara* leaves (Lauraceae *Cryptocarya* or *Endiandra* sps). An effect similar to the painted designs on *koem* was thus achieved in the medium of feathers and leaves.[32]

Peng kilt, as made by some of the Central Melpa groups,[33] required the services of a ritual specialist, whereas the other two types appear not to have done so. Such a specialist inherited appropriate spells from his father. He would comb out the wearer's hair, sprinkle it with softened *kilt* resin, and would then make his spell to ensure that the setting would be bright. With a brush of casuarina needles he shook liquid red ochre over the hair, to give it colour and make it attractive. He repeated this process several times in the ensuing days. After the resin had hardened, the hair had to be tapped loose again so that it could absorb each new application of ochre. The prospective wearers would stay in the men's house during the process of manufacture. They kept a pandanus mat at hand to protect the wig from possible rain while they were outside, and at night slept with a special raised head-rest.

These wigs required particular accessories. With *koem*, men wore a long apron, kilted up to facilitate dance movements (or they could don the shorter pig's tail apron, which we describe later); they had bustles of dried banana leaves which bounced up and down behind them (Pl. 59); and a plaque carved from white softwood on their foreheads. For their type of *kuklnga* the Northern Melpa wore an ordinary long apron with fur woven into its thread, along with a banana-leaf bustle. Face-paints worn with all three types of head-dress were bright: red, yellow, blue, and white with only a small amount of black charcoal. With *kilt* our informants mentioned that men also inserted tail feathers of the red lorikeet through their pierced nasal septum, and little pins of wood in holes pricked into the nasal alae, and wore cane bands round the arms and legs. (The last two features seem to be old-fashioned: only older men seem to have their alae pricked in this way nowadays, and cane legbands and armbands are regarded as archaic also.)

The *kilt* was donned for *ware*, a shuffling, twirling dance performed at pig-killing festivals. Dancers carried drums but not weapons, sustained themselves on specially cooked packages of greens and pig-fat which were supposed to 'make their skins good', and in their songs they called to the *kilt* and other flower-bearing trees, to light-coloured marsupials and to cool waters. The songs associated the dancers with bright shining things, in keeping with the emphasis on brightness in their head decorations; in fact, the objects called on are the same as those which appear in spells to enhance men's attractiveness. *Koem* could also be worn for *ware*, as for the similar *kng kui* dance. Both dances resemble those of the Wahgi Valley[34] speakers much more closely than do the *mør* and *kanan*.

Koem and *kuklnga* could be worn for rather a wide range of occasions, and we can best summarise these in a table. (Table 3.)

We mention here that in the Jimi Valley men used to wear a version of the *kilt* for everyday, not simply for dances.[35] This custom seems to link them to the near-by Maring, who wear their equivalent to *peng kilt* in connection with the dedication of young men to 'red spirits' associated with warfare, and in celebration of the killing of enemies.[36] To the main body of the Hageners, however, the meaning of *peng kilt* and the other wigs is quite different.

Although in making the head-dresses men had to conserve their male strength by abstaining from intercourse, the whole purpose of the finished product was to attract women. 'Only men make and dance with the *kilt* head,' a specialist remarked, 'for it helps men to get women. Women who watch the dance like its bright colour and come running to the wearer's house. It is the

89

Plate 59
Peng koem with its
banana-leaf bustle (but
no other accessories)

brightness of the *kilt* tree's red flowers which attracts flocks of birds to it, and
we attract women in the same way.'

    A stated aim of the *peng kilt*, then, is sexual attraction. This is effected through
an association Hageners make between a power to attract and qualities of
redness and brightness. By making the head-dress bright, they transfer this
power to it.

90

TABLE 3: *Contexts in which three types of head-dresses are worn*

Head-dress	Area	Dance and occasion	Other decorations worn
1. *Kilt*	A. Jimi	(Everyday wear)	(Everyday wear)
	B. Central Melpa	*ware*; pig-kill	Cf. text
2. *Koem*	C. Central Melpa	*ware/kng kui*; pig-kill	(a) Penambi tribe:[37] Red, White *kumin*, kilted apron, bustle
			(b) Yamka tribe: as (a) plus parrot, cockatoo, immature Princess Stephanie; fluffy eagle feathers down cheek; wooden forehead plaque
	D. Northern Melpa	*ware*; pig-kill *mør/kanan*; pig-kill	As for *mør* at *moka*, except that *køi wal*, eagle and *kumin* feathers avoided; cowrie baldrics popular in 1930s; apron could be kilted up
3. *Kuklnga*	E. Central Melpa	As for *koem*	As for *koem* except that unkilted apron and longer bustle worn
	F. Northern Melpa	*mør* at shell-*moka*	As for *mør* but without *køi wal*. (Worn by only two out of about fifty men on one occasion)

Note to Table 3

Bjerre (1964: between pp. 80 and 81) shows a picture of Hagen men wearing *koem* and *kuklnga* along with pig's tail aprons, and in one case with *køi wal*. Bjerre says that these decorations were for a 'ceremonial war dance', but in the absence of more specific information we cannot fit this into our account. Possibly the men were dancing at the Western Highlands District Agricultural Show held biennially at Mount Hagen township.

Koem and *kuklnga* (Central Melpa) could also be worn for the *Wøp* and related cults. See note 51 to this chapter.

This is achieved in several ways: men observe taboos which protect the wig from influence which might otherwise dull its appearance; a specialist pro-nounces spells during the manufacture to make the head-dress bright and shining; and red ochre is sprinkled over the hair, which Hageners see as having a bright as well as a red effect. These are all actions designed to create the desired qualities. In addition, resin from the *kilt* tree[38] is used in the manu-facturing process, and a further more general relationship is posited between the head-dress and this tree: the final appearance of the former is likened to the red *kilt* flowers.[39] These flowers in turn have powers of attraction which parallel the attractiveness Hageners say is produced by the bright red colour of the wig. The *kilt* tree is also named in the spell which the specialist recites: he lists all the birds which settle on its branches to 'eat' its blossom.[40] Men do not, however, wear the flowers themselves in this context; it is the resin from the tree which they employ.

We may briefly examine the logic involved, which in this case is made unusually explicit by Hageners themselves. The analogy between the head-dress and the *kilt* tree can be analysed in terms of a distinction (made by Tambiah)[41] between metaphor and metonym. On the one hand, through the quality of brightness and in particular the colour red, a similarity is seen between the head-dress and the flowers of the tree. Metaphorically, the head-dress has the power to attract women in the same way as *kilt* flowers attract birds. On the other hand, although the resin employed to set the hair is also from the *kilt* tree, it is the flowers of the tree and not the resin itself to which are attributed these powers of attraction. Nevertheless by association (the principle of contiguity) the resin can stand for qualities which other parts of the tree have, and when it is applied to the head-dress also transfers these qualities metonymically.

Brightness and redness are associated with powers of attraction, however, which do not necessarily depend on a further association with the *kilt* tree. Thus abstention from sexual intercourse preserves the fat, shining attributes of a healthy skin, these signs of health themselves indicating success; and red ochre has independent magical qualities of its own. Bright, red, and fragrant, it is regarded as a direct agent of attraction. We have, then, in the construction of the *peng kilt* head-dress a duplication of items which are magically bright and capable of attracting women.

A concern with the same qualities is also evinced in the making of *koem* and *kuklnga* wigs, which share with the *kilt* head attributes of attractiveness.

The element of secrecy in the construction of all these head-dresses is linked to this purpose of sexual conquest. Men explicitly say that when the wearers emerged from their seclusion place their aim was to surprise and frighten the women; but that after recovering from their shock, the girls would be delighted and run to marry the men.

At several points we have noted the attention given to enhancing the head in elaborate head-dresses. Wigs made of human hair are an essential component of this enhancing process. Apart from those made especially for an occasion, men build up wigs from clippings of their personal hair from adolescence onwards. Even young boys decorate their heads (cf. Pls 60, 61); youths wearing a wig for the first time oil it to make it attractive to women. Men take pride, too, in a luxuriant growth of beard. A good growth of hair – and it is this which the wig emphasises – is regarded as a sign of male strength. (By contrast, women's wigs made for *werl* are no more than supports for their feathers, manufactured from burrs held in place by netting[42] (Pl. 5). Women do not regularly keep their hair-cuttings to make wigs as men do.) Hageners express this idea of

Plate 60
Boys' hair is cropped short and they only play at decorating – imitation fur headbands of grass

Plate 61
Young men attend more carefully to their growing hair (see Col. pl. 27)

3

Plate 62
The swish of pig's tail
aprons

strength by saying that a man's closely related ghosts actually lodge in his hair, and that a good growth is evidence of their favour and support.

The especially large wigs we have been describing here are an expression of this attention paid to head-hair. When they are worn, feathers and other decorations take second place. They are painted in bright colours because the particular concomitant of male vigour which they are designed to celebrate is sexual attractiveness, which we have noted as one general aim of self-decoration.

The same stress on brightness is found in the special pig's tail apron (*kng øi mbal*). This consists of a number of pigs' tails sewn to a closely woven top part. When worn, the apron reaches no further than the knees. It seems to be used only for *kanan*; perhaps it would not suit the stately *mør*, in which aprons are supposed to sway in time with the plumes of head-dresses. Men say that they like to hear the pigs' tails swish[43] as they stamp out the *kanan* movement (Pl. 62).

Like all decorations, the aprons carry a message for the spectators; specifically, that the dancers are prosperous and have plenty of pig-meat to eat.

The set of ornaments worn with these aprons emphasises brightness. The apron itself is painted in red and white, and the dancers' legs and weapons are painted in wavy white lines. (This is done partly to keep the apron from being soiled by sweat or body-grease.) Above the apron the dancer tucks in a mass of light yellow *Miscanthus* inflorescence. On his head he wears a special wig-cover,[44] whitened with lime, which has a bark-cloth topknot painted red. He

94

has a single Red or perhaps White plume set on a hoop, flanked by Blue, capped with Saxony sprays, and fringed by narrow cassowary or cockatoo circlets at the back of the neck. Or instead of using feathers from the Blue bird, he may have made sticks from eagle breast feathers, white in colour (man on the left in Pl. 69). His cheeks are charcoaled to suit his beard, but his nose is red or white and he has white lines encircling the eyes or running across the cheeks, and perhaps a spattering of lime over his beard too. In addition, the relatively few feathers worn allow the white colour of the wig to be prominently exposed. Leaves, grasses, shells, and oiled back and chest complete the display[45] (Pl. 63).

At one dance[46] which we observed, perhaps half of the men wore this full

Plate 63
Whitened head-net, shiny bailer shells on chest and forehead and *Miscanthus* flowers top the apron

set of decorations; the rest lacked the pig's tail apron, and accordingly omitted the paint over the legs, the *Miscanthus*, and in many cases the whitened wig-cover.[47]

The pig's tail apron is especially appropriate to wear for pig-*moka*; so that we can summarise its salient associations by saying that it is worn for *kanan* dancing at pig-*moka*,[48] along with the whitened head-net and Red, Blue, and Saxony plumes. It is appropriate that pig-*moka* should be marked by white decorations. Hageners make a direct comparison between white, shiny orna-ments and the white pig-fat which they prize as food and use in the form of grease to anoint their skin. In spells they call on a range of white things, including shells, to make pig-fat abundant, since abundance of fat stands for health and fertility in general. Just as bright-coloured wigs make statements about sexual attractiveness, so the bright set of decorations which goes with pig's tail aprons conveys messages about health and prosperity. We may note here two emphases in the colour components of this quality 'brightness' – in the case of the wigs, a stress on the colour red; and in the case of the pig's tail aprons, the colour white.

Throughout all our descriptions so far we have found varying attention paid in the decorations to brightness on the one hand, and to darkness on the other. We pursue this theme further by looking at cult festivals and warfare decorations.

CULT DECORATIONS

We outlined in the previous chapter the rituals and dancing performed for the Female Spirit and *Wöp* (Male Spirit) cults, including the somewhat paradoxical point that the first is more exclusively an affair of men than the second.

For the Female Spirit cult no women take part as dancers (although some may partially decorate themselves as female visitors to a *moka*, as men who are not themselves dancing can do). The men wear the same whitened head-net which we have mentioned is worn with pig's tail aprons, but here it goes with the striped *mbal omb* apron (Pl. 38); White plumes (together with the Red, cf. Table 2); fluffy white eagle feathers arranged on sticks; glittering pearl shells which they hold in front of themselves while dancing; and large white bailer shells worn over the chest. The leaves employed as rear-coverings, too, are selected for their brightness, so that spectators will see them shining and shaking as the dancers stream out of the cult enclosure.

The emphasis on brightness is made explicit by the ritual experts. They tell the men they must put on bright things, and they make a spell to ensure that these will indeed be bright; and they forbid them, during the period of the cult, to employ poison, which, our informants explained, is thought of as black and associated with hostility and aggression. We may conjecture, therefore,

Plate 64
'Feather tower'
head-dresses

that blackness or dark things are regarded as antithetical to the white colour of the cult decorations.[49]

Decorations for the final dance contrast with those worn at earlier stages in the cult activities. A few months before the climax the cult participants hold a preliminary sacrifice inside their enclosure, and emerge with gifts of meat which they distribute to a wide range of visitors; and immediately before the last dance they sometimes make pig and shell-*moka* as well. For both of these events they wear only 'second-best' feathers – cassowary plumes. The important decorations are reserved until the last dance.

Why should there be an emphasis on whiteness in the ornaments for this cult? There seem to be hints in the explicit purposes of the cult itself. These are, as we have seen earlier, first to strengthen men against the weakening effect of menstrual pollution, and second to ensure that the earth will be fertile and people's skins will be good. If whiteness is connected with both these purposes, it would be a colour of both purification and fertility. Another component of its

Plate 65
Wøp cult: accompanied
by drummers, women
precede the main body
of male dancers

meaning seems to be revealed also: poison, associated with secret hostility, is referred to as 'black' and the white decorations thus seem to stress that the dancers are free from hostile intentions and hidden motives.

The *Wøp* cult is also concerned with fertility, but has quite different decorations. Both men and women dance at it.

At a performance held in the Nebilyer Valley during 1965 the men wore a standard set of *køi wal*, Saxony sprays, and long full aprons (*mbal omb*), with Enga wigs (Pls 41, 65). Their faces were charcoaled, with eyes picked out in white. They had large, mounted pearl shells over their chests, some set on a backing of lichen (said to be the custom of Tambul people, with whom the dancer's group had close connections), and forehead bailer shells flanked by fur; a number of men wore crescent pearl shells instead of the mounted ones. Important men displayed special sets of Saxony sprays branching from the sides of their *køi wal*: these were explicitly pointed out as marks of their status.

98

'Feather towers' (Pl. 64) were also worn (on this occasion only by a few boys, but they can be worn by men and women too): they consisted of a core of bamboo bound with bark-cloth and clad with light-red feathers, into which rectangular white and light-green insets were made. They had fluffy white feathers at the top, brown at the bottom. They were capped with two possum tails and a Saxony spray, and bound at their base with grey phalanger fur. So far as we could tell, they were not a prerogative of the sons of big-men.[50]

Apart from the special Saxony-spray arrangements, the men's decorations scarcely differed from those worn for an important *moka*. Similarly, the women and girls who danced were decked out as for *werl* dancing at a pig-*moka* (Pls 65, 79). They did not, however, follow the Kuli custom of wearing Princess Stephanie and Sicklebill feathers: instead they had a set composed of *kumin* (or a mass of eagle feathers) surmounted by fans of Red plumes and long white Ribbon-tailed Astrapia feathers. The wig made as a base for the women's plumes was the same as among the Kuli: a structure of burrs, held together by a net. After an initial parade the women in fact settled to a standard *werl* dance.

One young woman wore a *køi wal* (cf. Pl. 65) (as is apparently also accept-able for women performing *werl* and for girls dancing *mør* along with men). Male informants felt that there was some incongruity between the 'dark' *køi wal* and the bright red of the girl's face-paint, and suggested that she should really have charcoaled her face to suit the *wal*; 'but', they added, 'women don't like charcoal, they like bright paints, and we let them do this, since it is their wish.' This example is interesting from a number of points of view. First, it shows men commenting on decorations adopted by a woman and explaining that men and women have different preferences for face-paints. Second, it indicates that although the *wal* can be worn by women, when it is so worn an incongruity emerges between the dark effect of the *wal* and the bright paint ordinarily put on by women. Third, the incongruity is nevertheless allowed: no sanctions are brought to bear on women to make them wear charcoal. Indeed to do so would be against one of the implicit requirements of decoration, that men and women, although dressed similarly, should be distinguishable from each other. Finally, the example suggests an association between women and bright red face-paint.

If we follow through the implications of our discussion on decorations worn for the Female Spirit cult and on the special wigs and the pig's tail apron, one would expect that a cult such as the *Wøp* which stresses both fertility and sexuality would be marked by an emphasis on bright ornaments. Yet in the performance which we observed this was not notably so, at least for the men. We suggest that the basic reason for this is the requirement that men's decorations should contrast with those of women. The cult expresses fertility through co-operation of the sexes, symbolised by the act of burying cult stones in a position mimetic of copulation. Hence it is appropriate that both sexes should dance at it. As it is recognised that women wear very bright decorations, it is fitting for men to wear relatively dark ones, such as the *køi wal* and Enga wig. Moreover, the formal reason given for the patterns of male decoration at the *Wøp* is not that they are designed to attract women, as the brightly coloured special wigs are supposed to do, but simply that they indicate the men's strength and unity, which results from the cult rituals. Predominantly bright decorations would be less appropriate for conveying this message than dark ones.

Our explanation here is conjectural. It depends on two premises, first that the cult's logic requires both men and women to dance, and second that when both sexes do dance together the women wear the brighter decorations unless men are specifically dancing to attract sexual partners to themselves. The degree to which men and women are differentiated, and the items which discriminate between them, may well vary from one cult performance to another. Accounts of *Wøp* performances other than the one we observed suggest that in them the men's decorations were brighter.[51]

WARFARE DECORATIONS

All decorations worn for formal group occasions in Hagen can be described as epideictic:[52] they communicate to members of the group, and to outsiders, information about the strength of their wearers. They also set the occasion apart from ordinary, everyday life, and mark out certain men as members of a common group opposed to other similar groups.

In *moka* exchanges the relations between the parties are not simple ones of friendship or hostility but a combination of these two things, varying in emphasis according to recent political history. The emphasis depends on the scale of warfare between them in the past.

We must distinguish between minor and major warfare. The first took place between clans which periodically made peace with each other and conducted exchanges of valuables and women; the second occurred between whole tribes, aided by their respective allies, and was never effectively terminated by peace ceremonies and wealth exchanges. The former was described as *el øninga*, 'little arrow', the latter as *el parka*, 'Red bird of paradise arrow', from the fact that warriors wore *raggiana* plumes. In minor warfare, by contrast, few, or more often no decorations at all, were worn.

Here, then, the donning of decorations is associated with hostility between groups, and the more elaborate ornaments were worn in battles between groups which were in a permanent relationship of hostility.[53]

The details of the decorations for major warfare are as follows: a warrior would wear one or two feathers out of the following types: Red plumes split into two[54] and of an inferior, brownish-coloured kind, worn also as second-best for visiting; brown or black cassowary; yellow parrot wings; eagle; white cockatoo; Princess Stephanie and Ribbon-tailed Astrapia. For shell ornaments, pearl crescents, conus, and chest bailers were put on. Men regularly charcoaled not only their faces but also their whole bodies, and ringed their eyes in streaks of white or yellow, or put a white stripe down the nose. They pinned silver-grey Lauraceae leaves to their wigs, and in addition placed sprigs of it in their rear-coverings, sometimes together with a cane-leaf or banana-leaf bustle. On their foreheads they wore a carved softwood ornament, shaped either like a simple piece of bailer shell or like swiftlet wings. This last informants explained as a 'bad' item. The wooden replica was worn in place of the actual shell valuable, too precious to display in this context;[55] swiftlets can be birds of ill-omen, and they are said to be represented in this ornament because warfare is a 'bad time', a time of disruption and death.

As with *moka* decorations, there is a combination of light and dark items in the list. But Hageners emphasise that second-best plumes were the ones most regularly used, and that men would not wear a proliferation of items. Strictly practical considerations probably entered here: a warrior overloaded with decorations could scarcely be expected to move very efficiently, and there would also be a danger of losing valuable ornaments if a man was killed and his body despoiled. But informants go further than this, as their comments on the forehead plaque show: they state that warfare was a 'bad' (*kit*) time and therefore should not be marked by 'good' (*kae*) (i.e. new, abundant, and shining) decorations such as are suitable for a festival. Moreover, the brightest items displayed are spoken of as terrifying, not attractive, in this context. And, third, the warrior's whole body is charcoaled and this is said to have been designed to make him look large and frightening. Both bright and dark elements, then, are described as frightening in their effect here.

Glossy green leaves were not worn in abundance as they are for festivals: instead, the flat, whitish-grey Lauraceae, or dried grasses or banana leaves were used.

The most striking signifier of war, which differentiates its decorations most clearly from those for festival dances, seems to have been the blackening of the whole body with charcoal. We may adduce here the fact that warfare and poisoning were two alternative ways of carrying out aggressive action against enemies, and that as poison is thought of as a black substance, so black would appear to be an appropriate colour for warfare also. Just as poison was associated with secret motives and hidden action, so dark decorations were said to disguise the warrior as well as making him impressive. Further, darkness in face-colouring is also associated with the presence of helping ancestral ghosts, and these were held to accompany men into battle. The ancestors here are the totality of clan ancestors, so that what the dark faces of the warriors seem to be stressing is not so much their individual prestige, as in the exchange festivals, but their concerted, anonymous action on behalf of their clan with the aid of the clan ghosts.

Action in warfare was always supposed to spring from motives of revenge for some wrong done to the clan – theft of pigs or garden produce, seduction of women, killings, whether committed in open fighting, ambush or putatively by poisoning. We may perhaps, then, associate the wearing of black charcoal with a desire for revenge as well as with clan strength and aggressiveness.[56] If, however, a death was inflicted on them during the course of fighting, warriors returned home to mourn for the killed man, and when they took up arms again they smeared themselves in yellow and orange mourning clays, abandoning their wigs and other small items of adornment. This indicated that they were in a high state of grief, as well as anger, at their recent loss; and it was an appeal to their allies' sympathy, designed to make these come to their help in order to avenge the death.[57]

Warfare could thus lead either to loss of men, defeat and mourning, or to successful killings and victory, which would be followed by festival-like rejoicing. When victory was celebrated, warriors decked themselves out in better plumes, streaked their noses with bright red paint (where before they had worn white or yellow), and might even hold courting parties. Can we suggest, then, that the bright elements they wore for fighting represented their *élan* and confidence, and that this was why these bright things were supposed to be terrifying to the enemy? Such a conjecture is made more plausible by the fact that brighter objects were donned when success was actually achieved. Red ochre, in particular, is mentioned by some informants as being avoided during the time of fighting but put on for the subsequent celebrations. More confidently, we can state that the dark elements worn indicated anger, aggression, and the concerted efforts of the clan and its ancestors against the enemy: anger which could recoil into grief after a loss, when men displayed their bereavement rather than their aggressive confidence (grief at a death is said to make people physically weak).

Men decorated their weapons, as well as their bodies. Spear decorations, which were not elaborate, have already been mentioned.[58] It is particularly shields which we want to consider here. (We shall use the present tense in describing them, since a few are still in existence, mainly in museums. Most were burnt when the Administration stopped warfare, and since, unlike spears, they are never used for dances, no new examples have been made.)

A warrior's shield was almost like an extension of himself (and perhaps this is partly why shields were ornamented). Shields have a 'head' (their top) which is decorated with plumes, and their main surface is painted with designs which in appearance follow the patterns of those painted on cheeks (see Fig. 1).

The names of some of these designs are:

a. *Watinga:* a number of dotted-line marks, made with pointed flints, and resembling flecks on the pelt of the native cat,[59] *watinga.*

b. *Uklimb:* a circle or diamond painted in the middle of the shield, i.e. a navel, *uklimb.*

c. *Reipi ndum, reipi peng kela:* roughly triangular areas, rounded at the tips, done in red ochre (*kela*); described as 'forehead ornaments' (*ndum*) or 'red heads' (*peng kela*) of the shield (*reipi*).

d. *Kendepai pou:* two double chevrons meeting in the centre of the shield and dividing it into a number of distinctively painted panels: the chevrons were filled with white, the side-panels with black, and the top and bottom with red. The design was said to resemble swiftlet wings, *kendepai pou.* It is the same as that for the forehead ornament which is worn by the warrior.

e. *Pokan kuklumb waep:* designs resembling the sheath of the *pokan* shrub and the rounded leaves of the *kuklumb* plant.[60]

f. *Waep kerua:* chevrons, as worn on the face.

Kerua is the only one of these terms which is applied both to shield and face patterns. In the next chapter we consider face-painting and the actual designs involved; here we note that although the patterns may be very similar to those painted on the face, the terms for shield designs are on the whole different. Notably, nearly all shields have a 'navel' (*uklimb*), a concept inappropriate for the face, where we find similar geometric shapes called *nomong* ('pools of water'); the triangular effect of (e), when drawn for example down the sides of the nose may be called *porapaka* ('forked insect's tail'). In the latter case the preference for the different terms was not explained to us.

Actual shields combine these designs in double form or with various colour schemes. The dotted lines of (a) might trace the same overall designs as the painted ones, but the latter do not always follow the former exactly in their proportions. We may also note that (d), (e), and (f) are among several alternative designations for very similar patterns.

The head of the shield was decorated with plumes: cassowary, Princess Stephanie, split Red, and Ribbon-tailed Astrapia could be used, just as for the warrior himself.

The latent identification between the fighter and his weapons goes with the

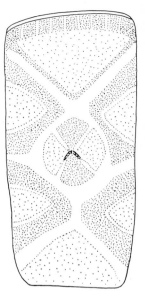

Figure 1
Wooden shield painted in white, red and black, now in the Pitt-Rivers Museum, Oxford. Height approx. 140 cm.

fact that weapon-making was exclusively men's business, just as warfare itself was. (Women could be killed, raped, or abducted in war, but they were not themselves expected to fight.) While making certain kinds of spears, or a battle-axe, or a shield, men were supposed to seclude themselves in a men's house and not have intercourse with their wives. It was feared that, should they do so, the weapons would be weakened: the axe would break, the spear splinter, the shield split. Shields might even be made far away from the home settlement, out in the bush or the forest, where suitable hardwoods were found and where women were unlikely to venture.

The general notion involved in these taboos is similar to that mentioned before in the section on the manufacture of special wigs: contact with women can jeopardise the efficiency of men's enterprises. We discuss the more specific logic of the ideas involved when we describe the importance of ancestral favour in the success of festivals (chapter six). Here we point out that an important component of this logic is the identification of the man with his weapons: if the man is weakened, which Hageners think is an effect of loss of semen in the act of intercourse, his weapons are made weak also.

Men decorated themselves for fighting at their own courtyards or a small ceremonial ground, and then gathered at their clan cemetery before setting out as a war-party. Women should not be present during the decorating and in particular could not go into the cemetery while warriors were preparing themselves there, in case they should step over a weapon and make it weak (here by direct influence, not mediated through an effect on the men). Ordinarily, women could enter cemetery-places, as when helping men decorate for festivals, but not when men were making ready for warfare. In the cemetery the warriors sacrificed a few pigs to ancestral ghosts before they left and prayed for success. Only men shared in this meat[61] – except that old women, who were past the menopause and therefore regarded as no longer dangerous to males, might be given a little. If a clansman were killed in the ensuing battle, it was to the cemetery that men brought his body back, and it was here that they plastered themselves with mourning clay, and made another sacrifice – this time including the newly dead man's ghost in their prayers, asking him to help them gain revenge.

Our description of warfare decorations and the ideas surrounding them helps to give us further clues to the interpretation of decoration as a whole. Warfare is a 'bad time', in that it can so easily lead to death and mourning; moreover, warriors are in general fighting to avenge wrongs and insults which make them feel 'bad' (kit). This association with death and revenge-anger explains why decorations worn for warfare are not 'good' (kae) as are those for festivals. War-decorations consisted of second-best plumes, and emphasised an overall dark appearance of the men's skins which is said to have disguised the warriors and made them frightening at the same time.

Yet despite this contrast between bad decorations for war and good ones for *moka* festivals, there are similarities between the decorations for both. Putting on ornaments (*moke*) at all in warfare was a form of display. At a *moka* men carry weapons, and their charcoaled faces are said to make them dark and disguise them. As we stated at the beginning of this section, *moka* prestations take place between groups which are partly friendly and partly hostile to each other; and *moka* dances are similarly displays of the strength of the donor clan and its opposition to the recipients, the emphasis on opposition varying in accordance with political relations between the two. It is true that exchange relations largely take place between minor and not major enemies, and that in minor warfare few decorations were worn, but it nevertheless seems appropriate that *moka* decorations should take over certain items used in warfare – charcoal and weapons – which express aggression (cf. Col. pl. 3). It is significant also that on the more important occasions, when the opposition of donors to recipients (or of both to a group of potential further recipients) is heightened, there is a greater stress on dark decorations.

Another theme in this chapter has been the importance of decorations in demarcating the statuses and roles of different groups and individuals at festivals, the different stages reached in a particular sequence,[62] and the different festivals themselves. The regular category distinctions which appear in festivals are those between donors and recipients, big-men and men of ordinary status, and men and women.

The first two distinctions are relative ones. There are no formalised offices of leadership nor any indigenous form of centralised government which could establish permanent relations of super- and sub-ordination in the society. Concomitantly, there are no items of ornamentation or 'regalia' which could belong to such offices and thus be the perquisites of those who held them. Individual big-men who have achieved eminence can display this by the wearing of numerous King of Saxony feathers and by an overall magnificence of their decorations. But they have no prerogative over these features. Other men are their rivals, and may supplant them as leaders: a big-man can decline in status and become like an ordinary man, whereas an ordinary man may rise to become a leader. Similarly, no group is permanently and unequivocally superior to another. Furthermore, the relations between groups are reversible: donors later become recipients of gifts from those to whom they first gave, cult celebrants later attend cult performances held by those who were spectators at their own, and so on. Indeed, it is precisely this process of reciprocity which maintains a rough state of equality between groups. Thus the individual or a particular group can experience a change of role: ordinary men can become big-men, donors can become recipients. The second experience is in fact a premise of the whole exchange system.

The same does not hold good for the category distinction between men and women; men do not literally become women, or vice versa, in the normal course of life,[63] nor in Hagen society is there any role which requires a person of one sex permanently or regularly to take on behaviour which otherwise belongs to the opposite sex, as appears to be the case for ritual specialists in some societies.[64] Again, there is no ritual which requires full transvestism on the part of either sex. It is in keeping with this that there are always clear diacritical features in Hagen dress which separate males from females, and that often the distinction is in fact a marked one. At a minimal level, the sexes are always differentiated by their head-nets, waist belts, and aprons, as well as by their own visible physical characteristics,[65] and almost always by their style of face-painting (although pre-adolescent boys, as we shall see, may have face-paint similar to that of women); and often they are distinguished by their precise arrangement of feathers and shells also.

The category opposition between males and females is an absolute rather than a relative one (as is that, for example, between big-men and others); and, as we have mentioned, the Hageners treat it as normally irreversible. Nevertheless, there is a certain parallelism in the qualities claimed, through the medium of decorations, by the sexes. In chapter seven we shall argue that while there is a predominant association of the sexes with opposite colour effects, there are also contexts in which men claim qualities which are regularly attributed to women and vice versa. This is not quite the same as role-interchange or transvestism between the sexes; but it may perform a similar function of partially neutralising what is otherwise a salient opposition.

CHAPTER FIVE

Face-painting

One of the ways in which men's and women's decorations are differentiated is by the adoption of different styles of face-painting. In this chapter, then, we discuss face-designs in some detail, to complement our account of feather head-dresses and wigs. The topic of face-paint also carries important clues for the interpretation of decorations as a whole, since it leads us into the theme of colour symbolism. Some colour associations are, as we have seen, made explicit by Hageners: red ochre is 'bright' and has magical powers of attracting wealth and women, for example; and white lime, when worn with the special pig's tail apron, is associated with pig-fat and wealth also.[1]

Designs painted on the face are named, and the terms indicate the way these designs are executed or their resultant appearance. Some examples of terms (illustrated in Fig. 2) are:[2]

1a. koemb kulya waep enem | he paints his nose

b. (i) kaem ketamin waep enem
   (ii) kaem ketamin ile enem | he paints his mouth with white clay

2a. kaem mong akenem | he excavates (i.e. encircles) his eyes with white clay

b. (kaem) mong akopa mintmint nonom | he encircles his eyes with spots (of white clay)

Figure 2
Illustration of some of the named types of face design (1a–3f). The sex of the wearer is not indicated (some of the designs may be worn by either sex, some by only men or only women)

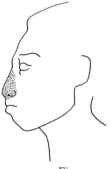

Figure 2, 1a

c. (mong akopa) kaklpa pokla ronom	(excavating his eyes) he cuts his face in half, i.e. makes a score across it
3a. kaem nggørman	pig's tusk of white clay (usually a diagonal line across the cheek)
b. kaem mokanøya	a bend of white clay like a bending branch (a curved streak across the face)
c. waep kerua	snake-skin paint (chevrons and interlocking diamonds)
d. ndamong mong waep	raindrops paint (streaks or dots)
e. waep nomong	water spring or pool paint (a diamond, square, circle, or lozenge; cf. *uklimb* on shields)
f. porapaka waep	insect with forked tail paint (i, forked design bridging the nose or ii, 'crow's feet' at edge of eyes; cf. *pokan kuklumb* on shields)

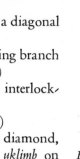

Figure 2, 1b

Note: a distinction can be made between the painted line and the area it encloses (Fig. 2). Thus: *koemb kulya ropa pondonom*, 'he paints the end of the nose'. This phrase is applied to the paint which fills in an area of the nose. *Koemb kulya kaklpa pokla ronom*, 'he cuts off the end of the nose', describes a line which separates one area of the nose from the rest of it. The line can also be referred to as *rur tinim*, 'he scores (the nose)' and *porapaka* (3f) (cf. Col. pl. 11).

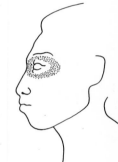

Figure 2, 2a

We can begin the analysis of these designs and the terms for them by saying what they do *not* do. Unlike feathers, they are not spoken of as unequivocally marking out the donors or other categories of male dancers at a festival (although they may indirectly have this function, see below). Nor do Hageners explain why their designs of category 2 emphasise particular parts of the face: they do *not* say, for example, that they encircle the eyes to enhance the attractiveness of these.[3] Further, the names of the designs do not carry any magical significance. The terms in category 3 are clearly metaphorical but they do not imply any magical transference of qualities between the object named in the metaphor and the wearer of the design, nor any attempt by the wearer to represent the object itself (e.g. a pool, raindrops, snake-skin, etc.): there is no overt reference in the names to things which are important in magic, mythology or ritual. Nevertheless, the designs *are* given names: they are items of decoration and can be listed along with feathers and shells. The names are mnemonics, which label the patterns used and enable them to be listed and stored in people's minds. Moreover, if we look at the empirical distribution of patterns worn by men and women (see Figs 5, 6), we shall find some differences between the sexes which

Figure 2, 2b

Plate 66
Face-painting requires
delicate care and
concentration

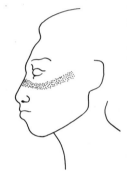

Figure 2, 2c/3b

parallel differences that appear in their other decorations also, and which link up
with the theme of colour symbolism.

First we must look at the list of design-terms in more detail, to see how the
terms relate to each other.

Terms we have grouped in category 1 refer to the general activity of painting;
those of category 2 detail a specific action; and category 3 terms describe the
effect of the designs metaphorically, commenting on their similarity in shape
to other objects – pig's tusk, raindrops, and so on.

At the most general level *waep* means simply 'painted pattern' or 'paint', and
the phrase *waep enem* ('he paints') can be applied to the painting of weapons and

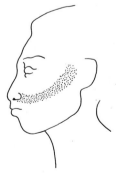

Figure 2, 3a

Plate 67
The face 'cut' by a white line

Figure 2, 3c

Figure 2, 3d

cult stones as well as of the face. It can cover all the terms we have given. At this level it can be modified by *kaem*, which specifies that it is white paint which is being referred to. *Kaem* can also occur by itself (cf. 1a and 1b). But at a lower semantic level *waep* may be used to contrast directly with *kaem* and to imply the use of bright colours other than white; this usage appears in category 3 terms.

At both levels of meaning *waep* implies that paint is applied carefully in order to enhance a person's appearance (Pl. 66). Smearing the body with clay, as in mourning (Col. pl. 31), is not regarded as making *waep*; and this technical distinction is reinforced by the fact that the clays and muds used in mourning are on the whole different from the pigments that produce *waep*. (*Kaem* is used for both decoration and mourning, but in the former case it is dried, powdered and applied to form particular patterns on the face, whereas in the latter it is plastered in wet smears all over the body.)[4] *Waep* is thus the execution of a design for decorative effect.

Figure 2, 3e

There is a further tendency to qualify terms which emphasise facial features with *kaem*, since these are most often done in white (such as ringing the eyes), while designs executed on the face as a simple surface (such as a chevron on the cheek) are referred to as *waep*; and this is relevant to the use of face-paint for distinguishing the sexes.

Phrases of category 2 can qualify those of 1, but their emphasis is placed more on the area of the face decorated, or on the effect of a line. Thus *mintmint* refers to a dotted line (Pl. 66), *pokla ronom* to the way the face seems to be cut in half by scoring a line underneath the eyes and across the bridge of the nose (Pl. 67). The verbs here contain metaphor: 'excavating' the eye, 'eating into (*nonom*)' the face with dots, 'cutting' the face.

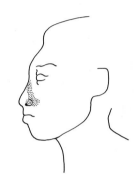

Figure 2, 3f(i)

Category 3 terms may overlap in reference with those of 1 and 2. Thus 2c and 3b are applicable to the same design, but 2c stresses the action of scoring and the visual effect of dividing the face in two, whereas 3b emphasises a curve in the painted line itself. The same curve, on the other hand, may be seen in lines which create a very different effect from 2c, so that 2c and 3b are not identical in their distribution. Again 3d taken as a whole is likened to the splashes of falling raindrops, but its constituent parts can also be described as excavating the eyes (2b) and painting spots on the cheeks.

Since there is overlap in the use of terms, and since the terms are based on broad visual similarities of the patterns to natural objects, observers may pick on different features in their descriptions depending on how they 'see' the designs. Variations in the way designs are executed can also lead to ambiguity: if 3b ('bending branch') is drawn very thickly in a prominent line that comes well over the cheekbones, it may be recognised as 3a ('pig's tusk') instead.[5]

Figure 2, 3f(ii)

III

What governs the choice of these designs for particular occasions? At dances it is obvious that each man tends to have some feature which differentiates him from the others or at least his neighbour, although such features may belong to his choice of feathers and shells as well as his face-paint designs (e.g. Pl. 68). But there are explicit limits on variation, set both by accepted cultural rules and by a value placed on overall uniformity which is affirmed at practice dances when men can see each other's styles of face-painting and can make mutual adjustments. Two or three young men from a single clan or sub-clan may decide to paint their faces in precisely the same manner and to dance close together, and a number of such small groups may increase the appearance of a standard face-design. Patterns, however, are not laid down by fiat of the big-men; nor are they the property of particular groups or individuals. They are not in any way exclusive identification marks. When men paint their faces alike they do so simply as an expression of friendship, and for a particular event. At other festivals they may decorate quite differently.

The chief agreed limits on variation are as follows. When men wear the *kφi wal*, they must charcoal their faces, and they should not have designs which are too bright, such as coloured chevrons. The latter are appropriate to a set comprising Red, eagle, and *kumin* feathers, worn at less important *moka* occasions or by helpers or recipients at a *moka* (Col. pl. 14). With *kφi wal* men should restrict their designs to white streaks or painted noses, which emphasise or do not disrupt the effect of the black charcoal base (e.g. 1a, 2a, 2b, 2c, 3a) (Col. pls 4, 9). But, within the range of designs appropriate to the *wal*, dancers can choose whether to divide the face, put dots or lines round the eyes, have a streak down the nose or a small blob of colour on the end, and so on. As we have seen,[6] a big-man may occasionally choose some unusual combination, in order to emphasise what he regards as his own uniqueness. This is a stylistic gamble which parallels other situations where big-men do 'outrageous' things. In the context of decorations the sanctions on this kind of behaviour are of two kinds: the gamble may not be greeted as successful, and the big-man thus stands in danger of losing rather than gaining prestige. Further, bad decorations are sometimes interpreted as a sign of disfavour on the part of clan ancestors (see chapter six), and no man wishes to appear to have incurred such disfavour.

The designs that tend to involve colour, rather than just white (although they may be combined with patterns in white, e.g. 3c, 3d, 3e), are not only more appropriate to the brighter *moka* decorations we have mentioned, but also accompany the wearing of 'judge's wigs' and *peng kilt*. Bright face-paint is also described as suitable for the Female Spirit cult; but when *kφi wal* is donned for *Wφp*, then the more restrained designs in white should be worn.

It is interesting, however, that there are no terms for particular combinations

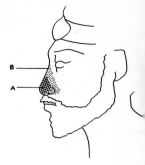

Figure 3
Relationship between two parts of a design
Stippling and hatching indicate two contrasting areas of paint.

A 'he paints the end of the nose'

B 'he cuts off the end of the nose' (i.e. outlines the coloured segment); this is also seen as 'scores down the side of the nose' and as the pattern 'like the forked tail of an insect'

Plate 68
Individual designs
chosen by Ndika
moka – donors

Plate 69
Girls dancing with men,
cheeks brightly adorned
with chevrons (R) and
lozenges (L)

Plate 70
Kuli wife's face painted in red, blue, white (Col pl. 24). Elements in the design of her face are shown in Fig. 4

of designs (see Figs 3, 4). Combinations do not become rigidly standardised and themselves given names as composite patterns,[7] which might then have been considered appropriate to a particular dance and have restricted person's choice of styles. The situation here is exactly analogous to the lack of overall terms for sets of feather decorations.

A further factor involved in the choice of face-decorations, as we have stated, is the wearer's sex (Col. pls 16, 17). We remarked that designs which follow facial features are usually done in white, while those in other colours can be located on an expanse of cheek, chin, or forehead. Certain of the former designs can be executed in colour as well as in white (for example 3a, as in Col. pl. 11)[8] but Hageners stress the use of white for them. This seems to be connected with the fact that patterns which pick out features are often (though not always) superimposed on a base of charcoal, the whiteness emphasising through contrast the black around it (e.g. Pls 32, 49). The coloured designs that men more rarely put on are applied to areas of the skin left free from charcoal, but although the dark effect is being played down here, we find that invariably men wear at least some charcoal along with the painted designs. Men, then, normally have a black base. It is the white rather than coloured designs which especially stress this blackness, and one could say that the combination of such a base with white lines emphasising facial features is particular to adult males (see Fig. 5).

Women, by contrast, wear a base of red (Col. pls 18–24). They may encircle the eyes in white as men do, and have lines or stipples radiating out from the eyes also (Pl. 56); but firm, white streaks seem to be particularly favoured by men (though see Pls 52, 70). We ourselves noted no examples of women using 2c (cutting face in half) or 3a (pig's tusk),[9] although there are possible cases of this in the literature on Hagen.[10]

Women tend to combine a red base with a number of brightly coloured designs of category 3 (e.g. 3c, 3d, 3e) and to use the whole surface of their face

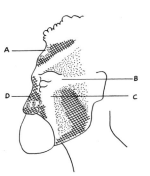

Figure 4
Colours are represented as follows:

hatching = red
stippling = blue
blank = white

A (forehead roundel)
  waep nomong, 'like an eddy in a stream, or a pool'
B (eyes outlined in white)
  kaem mong akenem, 'she excavates the eyes in lime'
C (white and blue streaks down the cheek)
  nde ndokl waep, 'like a vertically hanging tree branch'
D (nose painted red)
  koemb kulya waep enem, 'she colours the end of her nose'

Plate 71
Although wearing
køi wal, this unbearded
lad has his face painted
like a girl's

for these (see Fig. 6., e.g. Pl. 69, Col. pl. 21). Men recognise this explicitly, and explain that unlike women they have beards, which restrict the facial area available to them for painting. Their charcoal base is designed to emphasise the beard and the dark appearance which goes with it. (One part, however, which they often paint brightly is the nose, and this can be picked out in red and yellow as well as white. Only the tip of the nose is coloured in this way, so that the pigment does not cover a large area.) Women use chevrons and lozenges (e.g. 3c

116

Plate 72
Boy dancers, their
faces covered in *kerua*
patterns

and 3e) more lavishly than men (Pl. 69). Boys whose beard has not yet grown
follow the patterns used by women[11] (Pls 71, 72). These designs are often
executed on the cheek, but need not be confined to it. *Waep nomong* (3e) for
example, which can be outlined in one colour and filled with another, may be
painted by women on the forehead[12] and chin as well as the cheek (Col. pl. 26).

There does, then, seem to be an overall contrast between white, feature-
stressing 'male' designs, and bright-coloured patterns, painted on expanses of

skin, which women and boys favour. Both sexes regularly emphasise the eyes, men also highlight the nose, and women and boys colour their cheeks brightly (see Figs 5, 6). Any design combination can be broken down into elements that emphasise these parts.

For each area of the face there are several patterns which appear to be alternatives to each other, in a manner analogous to the distribution of allophones of phonemes and the complementary distribution of phonemes in a language. Hageners do not point to this themselves: we suggest it as an inference from our photographs of face-designs.

In languages, allophones of phonemes are in free variation: either can occur within an identical environment without materially altering the message which is being transmitted. On the other hand, if one phoneme is substituted for another, the message *is* altered. Analogously, we may treat the action of underlining the eyes as a 'picteme'. This action can be executed with an unbroken streak or else in dots. We could then describe the streak form and the stippled form of the design as allopicts of a single picteme. Or two more dissimilar patterns may be alternatives to each other in the same area of the face. Thus a man might paint either a pig's tusk line down his cheek or a chevron band: he wears one or the other, or if he has both they are named separately and regarded as different. The two designs would then be classifiable as discrete pictemes. But, as we already argued, there is no further explicit concatenation of patterns into sets, as phonemes are connected to form morphemes in the structure of a language. There is, however, an observed tendency for certain white designs to be worn most frequently by men and certain coloured ones by women.

A further contrast can be made between the handling of patterns by men and women. As we have noted, men stress that they are bearded, and that their face-paint should not clash too much with the dark colour of their beards. The beard, in fact, exercises a constraint over male face-painting as a whole. The moustache may be sprayed lightly with white, and the mouth rimmed, also in white, but facial hair is never painted with other colours (Pls 42, 63). A man who paints his cheek in colours applies a single pattern, so as not to overshadow his beard, whereas a woman may have several. If he encircles his eyes he does not usually extend lines in dots and streaks over his cheeks as a woman does;[13] and designs that men paint on their cheeks women often duplicate on their chins and forehead as well. Women's face-painting thus comes to give them a more lavishly and colourfully decorated appearance than the men's faces have. Their most elaborate and bright face-designs are worn along with the superabundance of feathers they don for the *werl* dance; but even if they are not otherwise fully decorated, as for the informal *mørli*, they may

118

Plate 73
Decorated *mǫrli* girls

still have brighter faces than the men. A phrase applied to women's face-paint indicates that Hageners themselves recognise this feature: women, it is said, *ui waep lil pakeremen*, 'put on colours in a slapdash (or profuse) way' (cf. Pl. 73).

We are thus suggesting a double contrast: men seem to prefer restrained designs executed in white, with only a limited area brightly pigmented in blue, red, or yellow; women choose lavish designs predominantly in bright colours, with only the eyes ringed in white. For men, we can say that an overall restrained effect is explicitly aimed at when both sexes are dancing together at a pig-moka or *Wǫp* cult. An overcrowded set of feathers or patterns is criticised when worn by a man; the same, or a greater, profusion is considered appropriate for women.

Another function of face-painting which we can deduce from variations observed at actual festivals is that it can modify the main 'message' carried by feathers.

For example, at the *moka* which men of two Kawelka clans gave to a pair of Tipuka clans in 1964 (described in chapter four), all the dancers tended to wear the same range of feathers. Among the donors, however, there was a tendency to do no more than pick out the eyes and colour the end of the nose, leaving the rest of the face black. Helpers and recipients from other clans, by contrast, had a greater variety of face-designs, and in particular painted their cheeks more profusely. Several of the younger men of these clans also had bright bands of colour across the bridge of the nose (Col. pl. 14). It may be remembered that we have suggested in chapter four that emphasis on dark colours in *moka* decorations indicates a measure of hostility towards other groups, and this fits our example. It is the *donors* at a *moka* who are particularly keen to justify themselves and to challenge the recipients; hence it is appropriate that the donors on this occasion wore fewer bright colours in their face-designs; while the all-round similarity in the feathers put on was consistent with the common interests of the participants and the fact that the occasion was not a full-scale, climactic one. We are not suggesting that the donors deliberately agreed to keep their faces dark in order to convey a note of aggressiveness. Nevertheless, the special uniformity of their face-paint was probably not accidental, for they had been practising in nearly full decorations for weeks, and there had been plenty of time and many oppor-tunities for them to confer on their styles and ensure that conformity was achieved.

The reverse of this example can also occur. At the 1967 Ndika *moka* (cf. chapter four again), donors and helpers were strongly differentiated by their head-dresses, despite the fact that they all belonged to the same clan. Donors wore *køi wal* and helpers *kumin* and eagle plumes. However, both donors and helpers had rather bright face-paint and were not distinctly differentiated in terms of this. Donors were marked only by tending to have a streak across the cheek as well as under the eyes (Col. pl. 11). Nearly all of the men had red noses, sometimes further picked out in yellow and white (Col. pl. 15). The face-paint of the men thus seems to have linked donors and helpers together, although their feathers differentiated them. Perhaps, also, by its touch of brightness it relieved the dark effect of the *køi wal* – which was somewhat unusual for an occasion when so few men danced.

In the first example, then, face-paint distinguished donors from helpers and recipients; in the second it equated them, in both cases cross-cutting the messages conveyed by the dancers' feathers.

Face-paint may also state a message less ambiguously than feathers do. An instance is the plume-arrangements which women at the Kuli *moka* of 1967 wore. They were distinguished from the men's head-dresses by their brightness and profusion. Yet this profusion was also said to 'darken' the women's appearance and thus to make them more like men.[14] In such circumstances the brilliant red base to their face-paint, which women had, unambiguously

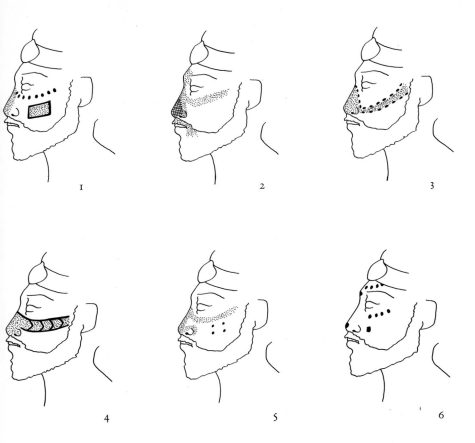

1   2   3

4   5   6

Figure 5
Examples of men's
decorated faces

1–6
Taken from observed
instances of the face-
painting of adult men.

Stippling and hatching
indicate areas of
colour/lime; unbroken
strokes solid lines of
paint; the use of specific
colours is not indicated.
The designs would be
executed on a black
base.

121

Plate 74
The pattern called
nde ndokl waep (talcum
powder on cheek and
chin adds an individual
touch)

differentiated them from men, and indicated that the dominant effect aimed
at for women is brightness rather than darkness.[15]

The Kuli women's eyes were encircled, and blue and white streaks ran from
the lower edge of the circles down the cheeks, in the shape (Pl. 74) called
nde ndokl waep ('hanging tree branch') or *ka kon waep* ('furrow made by falling
tears'), or also *rur waep* ('an incision', such as is made in cutting meat). Women

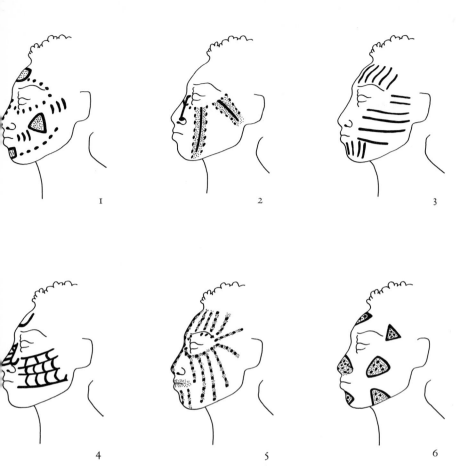

Figure 6
Examples of women's
decorated faces

1–6
Taken from observed
instances of the
face-painting of women
and girls.

Convention as in Fig. 5;
the designs would be on a
base of red paint or else
on unpainted skin.

123

differed in individual details – whether a line was dotted (Pl. 74) or unbroken (Pl. 70), whether a circle round the eye was starred or not – but the general patterning employed by all the female dancers was very similar (cf. Pl. 56). The men on this occasion were 'dark', since the festival was treated as a dress-rehearsal for an important tribal event, and it was noticeable that donors and recipients alike (again distinguished by their feathers) all had heavily charcoaled faces (cf. Pl. 55) picked out only by streaks of white and small blobs (in many cases also white) at the very tip of the nose (Col. pls 4, 17). They thus tended to stress both restraint and darkness of decorations, while the women were flamboyant in lavish and colourful ones.[16]

The example underlines our opening point in this chapter, that face-paint often contrasts the sexes. Men choose charcoal, women red ochre as a base (except in reversals of the ordinary decorative situation, for example when women wear charcoal in the 'netbags of greens' ceremony described in chapter three).[17] Even when women display *køi wal* they refuse to wear a charcoal base, since 'they prefer bright colours', as Hageners say. Similarly, Hagen men stick to their charcoal[18] unless they are specifically imitating customs of the Wahgi Valley men of Banz or Minj (when they shave off their beards as well to make room for brighter paints) – for example, as when R^e^mndi[19] men performed a Banz style *kng kui* in 1964.

Our discussion of face-paint thus brings out a number of points. Painting is not haphazard: there is a pool of named designs, some of which are usually executed in white, others in colour. White designs on a charcoal base are favoured by men, and these particularly suit the *køi wal* and a dark Enga wig; whereas women favour bright cheek patterns. Face designs can also separate donors from others, or link donors and helpers together, or equate all the men by contrast with women. In doing so the designs and colours can modify the message carried by dancers' head-dresses, either by emphasising an overall 'dark' or 'bright' effect already present in the feathers and other ornaments, or by stressing qualities opposite from those marked by the feathers – as when they link donors and helpers who are separated by their plumes, or distinguish men and women, whose decorations can both be looked on in a sense as 'dark', by making the women unambiguously 'bright'.

CHAPTER SIX

Reactions to display: the meaning of decorations

In the two previous chapters we have described the sets of decorations worn by donors and recipients and by the sexes at particular festivals, and have shown how the decorations differentiate categories of dancers from each other, especially in terms of the overall 'dark' or 'bright' effect of their costumes. In this chapter we discuss the reactions of spectators to displays in rather more detail than we have given so far, as a prelude to examining further the question of the meaning of decorations.

REACTIONS

In a world of competitive clans epideictic displays such as those we have been describing in this book are very important: they are the major arena for ritualised competition between groups and individuals. In festivals, then, competition is played out in a variety of modes. It may be in terms of sheer numbers of men dancing: one tribe, through its big-men, will challenge another to bring its members, and the two will line up to see which group has the most. But this rather crude and direct method is not the one most regularly chosen. More often competition centres on the size of the prestation being made and on the quality and arrangement of the dancers' decorations. There is some rivalry among the members of a single group as to who can accumulate the most magnificent set of ornaments, but the competition is also turned outwards: donors are vaunting themselves before recipients, and all the dancers are challenging the spectators in general to match their splendour when they, too, come to stage displays.

In *moka* the donors' explicit aim is to cap the previous gift of valuables, which they received from the group now their recipients, with a number of extra gifts which will enable them to 'win', and thus to draw admiration from the spectators as a whole. They can achieve this only if their decorations as well as their gifts are excellent. There is a custom of paying men from other groups who attend in order formally and publicly to praise the festival being held. Shells and plumes for those who give praise in this way may be held up by the donors at the end of the dancing.

Payment for praise implies that the spectators' reactions are valued; and the same conclusion emerges from other pieces of evidence. Thus, in accounts of cults or *moka* at which the donors appear from behind an enclosure, what informants stress is that the waiting crowd should be struck by the dancers' appearance – by the mass of gleaming white plumes, head-nets and pearl shells in the Female Spirit dance, for example. Few informants know or bother about esoteric reasons for particular cult ornaments, as in this case the point that whitened head-nets resemble spiders' webs which are supposed to be wound round the Spirit's own head when she appears to men in dreams. Instead they emphasise that ornaments are worn to make the crowd cry out and admire them. In fact the donors emerging from the cult enclosure are themselves treated as the Spirit, for as they appear the crowd shouts, 'The Spirit is coming.'[1]

The reason why such care is given to decoration is even clearer in the case of the large painted wigs made for pig-killing festivals. As we have seen, they were constructed explicitly to astonish, delight, and attract women. Sexual attractiveness is also aimed at in other festivals, too: at any dance women may watch individual male performances with a critical eye, and if they praise a particular man he should make them a small private payment (in money, a knife, a mirror, etc.). A girl compliments a *mør* dancer by joining in at his side (Pl. 75) and spending a night at his settlement (although not, in theory, at his house) afterwards. When a senior kinswoman comes to collect her, the man pays the girl a shell, beads, or money for the compliment.

There are definite canons by which spectators make judgements. Dancers doing *mør* must keep their backs straight, and they should bend their knees in proper time with each other. A correct, forceful movement produces a sweep of the long apron and a sway of the high plumes. When judging the actual decorations, spectators take into account the appropriateness of the dress for the occasion; the quality of the items – for example, blue wool is not wholly acceptable as a substitute for Blue bird plumes; the personal excellence of individual turn-outs; the degree to which members of a group have co-ordinated their decorations; and the skill with which elements have been combined – for example, one of the reasons given for why women rarely wear *køi wal* is

126

that its dark effect does not suit women's brightly painted faces: this was the point of criticism which men made in discussing the *køi wal* a girl wore at the *Wøp* festival we described in chapter four. Men may similarly be criticised for not charcoaling their faces heavily enough to go with their other decorations, or for allowing their features to be recognised easily; and women may be praised, as we have seen, for wearing a profusion of really bright items.

In addition, as we mentioned in the first chapter, people are conscious of cultural and sub-cultural differences in what is considered appropriate festival attire (they have probably become more aware of these differences since the cessation of warfare and the introduction of road transport). Men point to differences between their own decorations and those of other groups within Melpa and Temboka areas, as well as those of other related Highlands peoples. Visitors from distant areas watching a festival may, in fact, disparage a display which lacks some component they value. Their criticism is in this case directed not against individual performers but against the whole region they come from.

This perception of cultural differences can be illustrated very clearly from

Plate 75
Girls may join the men they admire

127

remarks made by one of our chief informants among the Northern Melpa, on the Kuli *moka* (Eastern Melpa, cf. chapter four). He did not see the event himself, but made his judgements on the basis of photographs which we showed him afterwards.

His first comment was that the decorations of the Kuli women and girls differed from his own area's custom: 'They have circlets of *kumin* feathers;[2] they wear white marsupial furs wrapped right round their foreheads and they mount the Superb bird on their foreheads too; their Red bird plumes are raked forwards in the manner of the Wahgi Valley; and they have parrot feathers running down their cheeks (cf. Col. pl. 22) – where our women wear only nicked-out *kumin* feathers. All these features relate them to the Minj people just to their east – the people whom we speak of as wearing whole parrot wings over their cheeks, whereas we [i.e. Northern Melpa] do not.'

These neutral observations were continued with remarks on the men: 'Some of the Kuli men wear flowers as a base for their forehead shells of green-snail, whereas we wear only *malt* [a type of pine] leaves. Some have whole spitted lorikeets or yellow parrot wings[3] (Pl. 50). Although they are wearing Enga wigs, they combine these with red parrot feathers, as well as with Princess Stephanie plumes. The latter they also wear along with Sicklebill tails as an alternative to *køi wal*. Perhaps all this is Minj custom too. We do not do these things.'

Finally, he made more critical judgements: 'Their aprons are too small and their wigs are too large. One has a long marsupial tail over his chest, the kind of thing which can be worn everyday by men, as well as women, but not for dances.[4] One has fern and pine leaves at the front of his apron, whereas these should be at his back. And look! One is actually wearing coffee-tree leaves in his rear-covering [clearly a piece of innovation]. Doesn't he know that this is not done?'

The speaker thus moves in his comments from instances of custom which he recognises as different from that followed in his own area to judgements on the shape or placement of ornaments, and here he becomes less favourable. A similar note of disapproval, indicating rivalry, is sometimes struck in turn by Central Melpa people commenting on the Northern Melpa. One person, for example, claimed that Northern Melpa do not charcoal themselves properly, do not know all the *moka* customs since these were invented in the Nebilyer Valley far away from them, and so on. Conversely, our Northern Melpa informant, in looking at pictures of a *moka* in the Nebilyer Valley itself, noted that the dancers lacked sufficient green leaves and grasses to make themselves look 'bright and fresh'; whereas Northern Melpa men, with easy access to high forest areas, pride themselves on having an abundance of plant decorations.

In addition to picking on these details at a given time, people are aware of changes in fashion over time, and have a definite concept of giving up certain customs and adopting new ones.[5] Europeans have in the past thirty years had a considerable effect on decorations, and many of the fashion changes seem to belong to this recent period.

First, Europeans made it possible for Hageners to intensify the scale of their decorations. Planters, missionaries, and Government officers brought in thousands of shell valuables,[6] and Hageners responded by wearing and giving away increased numbers of these at their festivals. In the late 1930s women sometimes danced completely swathed in baldrics of cowrie ropes, or wearing a whole chain of pearl shells reaching from the neck to below the knees.[7] These are no longer seen, except in fringe parts of the Hagen area. Fewer cowries, and a single shell, mounted or not, are nowadays preferred.

Indirectly, Europeans also exercised a selective influence. They inflated the shell currency, as we have noted, and certain types of valuable went out of popularity, notably cowrie ropes and nassa mats, which women used to wear. On the other hand, the smaller nassa headbands have remained fairly popular among men, as have conus and bailer shells. Perhaps this might suggest to us that women's ornaments are more directly regarded as displays of wealth objects, pointing to the wealth of their men.

More recently, some Europeans have introduced a directly suppressive influence. Men sometimes say that in general they do not decorate themselves as much as they used to, because they are ashamed before the Europeans. This 'shame' has two aspects: Hageners are perhaps ashamed of what they consider as wealth, in the face of Europeans' superior possessions; and, second, puritanism is involved, particularly where the Lutheran Mission is concerned: baptised men are expected to take up European clothes and to forsake moka-making and polygyny. Local Government Councillors are also expected by European Council Advisers to change from traditional dress, and to wear clean shirts, shorts, and, nowadays, shoes; although Councillors are not forbidden to decorate in traditional style at festivals, and may still do so (cf. Pl. 76).

Last, in recent years European traders have had a substitutive influence on decorations, associated with the spread of roads and stores and the acquisition of money through plantation work and cash cropping of coffee. Beads, armbands, bangles, rubber rings, and belts of leather, plastic, and beadwork can be worn instead of or along with traditional cane ornaments (e.g. Pls 24, 25). Girls put on bright red trade-cloths in a variety of styles[8] instead of netbags and head-nets – or together with these. Their strands of beads replace cowrie necklaces (Pl. 77); they have rubber rings on their wrists where before they wore pig penises (e.g. Pl. 81). Coloured paper is used to give a bright effect: men pin fish-tin labels to their foreheads, or cut-out circlets from Player's cigarette packs which they stick on to their forehead bailers. At one *mɵrli* dance we saw a girl wearing a City of Adelaide pennant between her breasts instead of a marsupial tail.

Europeans have also probably facilitated the diffusion of decorative items and styles from one area to another, since men now travel and see more of one another's festivals. The Rᵉmndi tribe in 1964 learnt special pig-kill dances from Banz experts whom one of their big-men had met while working near to the Banz area. The spread of Enga wigs may have been accelerated by better communications also. However, cults, dances, decorations (and many other kinds of custom) have probably been transferred from group to group in the more distant past also, before Europeans came.

In this section we have shown how spectators react to and judge decorations at a dance and how details are picked on as indicating cultural differences or as matters for adverse comment. Informants have clear ideas of what is appropriate for a given dance or festival in their own area, and can contrast this with customs of other groups. In comparing their own ways with those of others they usually manage to inject a little scorn into their accounts – which reminds us of the premise with which we started: that decorating is essentially a competitive business.

MAGIC AND THE INVOLVEMENT OF GHOSTS

To praise or disparage a group's display is not simply to pass an aesthetic judge-ment. A group's success on the occasion of a festival has for Hageners further very important connotations. A clan can achieve success only if it has the active support of its ancestral ghosts. The deceased forebears of a clan are felt still to be members of it and to care for the fortunes of their descendants. At a festival, a demonstration that an individual or a group is prosperous and healthy itself indicates ghostly blessing. Conversely, failure or disaster is a sign that the ghosts have become angry at some wrong and have withdrawn their help.

Although deaths are often spoken of as caused by ghostly attack, the ghosts attack only if they are offended. They are said to be as concerned for the success of a clan's enterprises as the living clansmen themselves are, and are considered to help it in *moka*, cult performances,[9] and warfare. What annoys them is a moral misdemeanour which disrupts relations between clansmen or between living men and themselves: just as clansmen must maintain relationships by gift-giving, so ghosts require sacrifices.[10] Hence we find that, to ensure ghostly favour, sacrifices must be made before an important display. For minor or preliminary festivals, sacrifice is not so crucial, since prestige is not so strongly at stake; but at a climactic festival prayers and sacrifices should always be made.

Plate 76
Traditional and modern dress on election day

In the past these took place in clan cemetery-grounds, and it was there also that men put on their decorations. Nowadays, through mission influence, such activities are much truncated, and people decorate themselves in the court-yards of the men's houses or at ceremonial grounds themselves. Nevertheless, the meat cooked for visitors and persons who help with decorations is itself a sacrifice to enlist ancestral support, although it is no longer overtly accompanied by prayers.

It may be remembered that this pig-cooking prior to a dance is particularly necessary if men are to wear *køi wal*, since they must pay those who have brought them the special Saxony plumes. But it is necessary also in a deeper sense, for if dancers attempted to don these plumes without a sacrifice, even if the feathers were their own, it is feared that they would be dull, the men themselves would look thin, and their performances be a failure.

A household head would make some prayers on his own behalf at a sacrificial hut in his settlement, directing the prayers perhaps to a dead father and to ghosts on his maternal side as well. There would be a further communal sacrifice in the clan cemetery at which a big-man of the clan prayed to the general body of clan ancestors, asking for the success of the group as a whole.

In addition to these prayers a specific ritual used to be performed, which was designed to make *køi wal* head-dresses appear shining and new (although *køi wal* are 'dark' by comparison with other feathers, they must still look shining rather than dull, and in this sense one can say that the ritual was to make them 'bright'). On the day before a dance, men built an enclosure at the end of the ceremonial ground which backed on to a cemetery-place. There they cooked pigs in sacri-fice. If the meat was amply sufficient, this was taken as a sign that the group would increase; if not it was a sign that some of their number would die. A ritual expert[11] took leaves of a plant *kengena* (Urticaceae *Elatostema* sp.), which is regarded as especially 'fresh' (*mel kont, mel kundil ninim*), dipped the leaves in a mixture of water and fat, and asperged the *køi wal*, to make them shine. At the same time he spoke a spell to ensure clan prosperity and success in dancing: its men should be big, fat, and healthy, and after the festival their pigs should continue to multiply, so that later they could make *moka* again.

Although this ritual has now been abandoned, the ideas behind it are still operative, and it is very important for a group to have good decorations. Shabby, dull ornaments would mean that the clan has been unsuccessful in securing the help of its own ghosts as well as failing to obtain help from friends and kinsmen, and this in turn is taken as a sign that further ill-luck will follow. A display that is a failure (or even one washed out by rain, for this too is an indication of ancestral disfavour) is said to forbode a death; whereas if decorations are splendid, this implies good luck for the future also.[12]

132

Plate 77
Between a conus shell nose-piece and bailer pendant, swathes of trade-store beads. (In contrast with the *morli* girls behind, this dancer is heavily oiled)

Dances express desires for health, strength, fertility, prosperity. At the same time, they are demonstrations to the outside world that these desires have been attained, both by the aid of spirits enlisted in ritual and by the dancers' own economic efforts. Decorations at the dances carry both of these purposes: to attract future prosperity and to demonstrate it in the present.[13] In the past such displays carried messages to the group's war-allies and enemies about its wealth and strength.[14] Nowadays, when warfare is suppressed, no group is in danger of being exterminated through war, but rivalry has been rechannelled into the exchanges and dancing displays themselves. Indeed these are now the only medium in which group rivalry can be fully expressed.

Since dancers claim present prosperity and well-being, it is consistent that individuals who have suffered some recent misfortune refrain from joining in. This is particularly likely if they have been ill and have become thin, or if they have suffered a bereavement. Indeed, should one of their men die, the clansmen will delay celebrations, both because they are mourning and do not 'feel good', as dancers must do, and because the death is in any case a sign of ancestral displeasure which would make any attempts at display unsuccessful. Sometimes the close relatives of a big-man who has died will refuse to dance at all for several years, simply because they 'feel bad' and are still mourning for him. Under such circumstances they could not contemplate dancing, for self-decoration is the antithesis of mourning. In mourning the body is neglected, dirtied, even mutilated by the tearing-out of hair and the amputation of finger joints; by decoration it is enhanced and made attractive. In Hagen thought material success and physical health are alike expressed in a man's bodily condition. A person should be well filled-out, with a gleaming skin, and oiling the body contributes to it a desired, glossy appearance (Pls 77, 78). Hageners also say that one of the aims of decorating is to make the dancers appear larger: at festivals, where they wear a whole range of ornaments their enhanced size goes with an increased attractiveness; in warfare it makes them impressive and frightens the enemy.[15] Thus, at festivals ancestral ghosts are prayed to not only to ensure that decorations will be good but also to make the dancers themselves appear strong and beautiful.

From one point of view, then, the whole act of self-decoration is a kind of omen-taking. Decorations cannot be worn successfully without ghostly support; in turn such support can be effectively demonstrated only by wearing good decorations. Actual omen-taking in the past accompanied the removal as well as the preparation of *kǫi wal* head-dresses. The dancers retired behind the enclosure next to the cemetery, and as each man took off his head-dress the ritual expert threw charcoal in his face: if a piece lodged in a man's eye, it was a sign he would suffer misfortune. Both entry into and exit from the proud state of

Plate 78
Oil adds a final gloss to the attire

dancing was marked by ritual to test whether each man was favoured by his ancestors or not.

Although a poor general display implies that ghosts have withdrawn their support, dull ornaments and a weakly appearance in male decorations may also be a result of the harmful influence of women, as we have mentioned in earlier contexts.

A taboo which men should observe throughout the period of decorating and dancing underlines the necessity for men to be strong and to make a good impression: they should not have sexual intercourse at these times. Breaking this taboo, it is said, would have three results: first, men would have no luck when they hunted in the forest for marsupial furs or plumes for their ornaments; second, their decorations and face-paint would be dull and hence ineffective; and third, their flasks of oil or pig-grease would run dry when the time came to anoint their skins for the dance – it is said, in fact, that the grease would dry up in the same way as men's skin becomes dry if they eat food which has been contaminated by the hands of a menstruating woman.

All three unfavourable results depend on similar ideas. The first issues from the notion that, in order to obtain things in the forest, which is the domain of dangerous wild spirits, men must be particularly strong, and intercourse would weaken them, both through loss of semen and through possible pollution resulting from sexual contact. The second and third examples can be interpreted in more than one way. Either we can say that males are afraid they might inadvertently transmit some piece of menstrual dirt, acquired during intercourse, to their decorations and grease-flasks, which would render these dull and dry; or we can posit that an intermediate step is present in this logic: men are weakened or polluted by intercourse, and their decorations and flasks are spoilt because these are regarded as in a sense extensions of the men themselves – men and their decorative items are identified. In the case of grease-flasks such logic would make good sense: the grease in the flasks is identified with semen and with the 'grease' that Hageners point to as making their skin appear healthy and fat rather than dry; so that, if the men lose semen and their skin condition becomes poor, this will affect their grease-flasks also.[16]

It is possible to offer these alternative accounts of the underlying logic of Hagen ritual practices because Hageners themselves are not entirely explicit on such matters. However, the general import of the taboos on intercourse at the time of dancing seems plain enough: men must not dissipate their sexual energies but conserve them in order to make a fine display.

There are three components in the Hageners' attitudes to women which are relevant here. The first is the general notion that females have a weakening influence: too close an association with women debilitates a man. Men are especially vulnerable to their influence in times of war-making, and no women, as we have seen, was supposed to be present when men made weapons or decorated themselves for warfare in clan cemeteries, in case they should weaken the fighters' spears and shields. This general notion is, of course, closely connected with and issues from the two more specific ideas that in intercourse with women men lose semen and are thereby weakened; and that, in addition, female menstrual fluids are positively dangerous to males. One of the functions of the Female Spirit cult, as we have noted, is to purify men from female contamination. In everyday affairs, a woman who is menstruating or who has recently given birth to a child (which puts her in a similar condition) has to avoid her menfolk, since contact with her would pollute them. For the same reason, although wives could ordinarily accompany their husbands into the cemetery to help them decorate for an exchange festival (not warfare), a menstruating woman could not do so. Nor would a menstruating woman herself decorate or participate in dancing. There are sanctions here: in general she would make any feathers she touched or wore dull, and more specifically the oil in her own flasks as well as those of her husband would dry up.

When women danced, they did not in the past make sacrifices to ghosts on their own behalf.[17] Access to the ancestors was controlled by men. Moreover, when the ghosts were called on, it was particularly to impart strength to the male dancers. It is not only that the influence of the ghosts is shown through the effectiveness of decorations: ghosts are thought actually to be there, accompanying the men. Two attributes of male decorations signify their presence: wigs and charcoaled faces. Hageners say that their ancestral ghosts sit in their hair and make it grow abundantly. Sometimes it is simply the size of the head and its hair which is emphasised, and the hair is covered by a net; at other times the wig is uncovered and moulded into a style such as the Enga 'head', and its black gloss may be brought out through sprinkling oil on it (Col. pl. 15). Wigs and, of course, beards are typical of men rather than women; only males wear large wigs when they decorate themselves.[18] Second, the base for men's face-paint is invariably charcoal, at least around the area of the beard. Hageners not only say that charcoal suits their beards but also that a dark effect throws the face into shadow and disguises it, and that under these circumstances spectators comment, 'Their ancestors have come on to their faces and they are dark in appearance.'

We have mentioned the same aim of disguising the wearers in the case of warfare decorations. Why should participants at festivals be disguised? We suggest that what is being expressed here is that the identity of the individual dancer is partly submerged with that of the rest of his clansmen in the creation of a group display (we say 'partly' because we know that in fact dancers are also

137

implicitly competing with each other as individuals). In a sense Hageners put it like this, too, in saying that the dancers are in shadow because ancestral ghosts have 'come to their faces'. It is the presence of the ghosts that links men together as clansmen and gives them a common identity. The living men are representatives of the clan as a corporate body, whose interests are presided over by the dead members of the corporation. It is in a very real sense that Hageners speak of the living and the dead men of the clan dancing together. Similarly, ghosts accompany charcoaled clansmen when they go out to do battle against enemy clans.

Hageners do not rely exclusively on ancestral help for success in competitive activities. They also use magic, specifically, as we have already indicated, the recitation of spells.[19] In these, men call on things which embody the qualities they themselves desire: for example, bright-flowering trees which attract birds (in the same way, men hope to attract women), and birds of prey which find plenty of meat (in the same way, men hope to obtain wealth objects). In some contexts spells are recited by ritual experts, as when especially elaborate decorations such as the *kilt* wig are made, and when *køi wal* are to be worn. But the whole logic of self-decoration can itself be seen to follow that of spell-making.

Just as spells call on things and harness them by the power of words (through metaphor), so the actual wearing of items of decoration can magically promote the wearers' desires (by metonymy – they become as strong or attractive as the birds of prey or the *kilt* tree by donning a *part* taken from them).[20] Men will thus be as powerful as the things they wear. Hageners do not state this as a general point; but it emerges clearly enough from examples. We have mentioned the *kilt* wig; we may cite also the pig's tail apron (its wearers will be as healthy, they say, as the white fat of their pigs which they represent in their dress), and the use of red ochre (while its colour attracts girls, pigs and shell valuables are said to 'follow' the ochre's fragrant smell). Oil and grease are highly symbolic, too, as we have seen: they imply a healthy sheen on the skin, strength, and sexual attractiveness.

Decorating also includes the wearing of actual valuables (Pl. 79, Col. pl. 6), pearl shells, bailers, conus, cowries, etc., and although the number of such valuables which a man dons bears no realistic relationship to his own wealth and social status – the bamboo tally stick recording the shell-*moka* transactions a man has made is a closer indicator of status, and this can be worn every day – wearing items of intrinsic value is held also to attract further wealth. It is interesting to note here that successful operators in the *moka* system depend a great deal on credit, and one way of maintaining confidence in their ability to meet creditors' claims would be precisely to put on a good display at a festival.

Plate 79
Women wear their
husbands' wealth (*Wøp*
cult)

Not only is there a parallel between the use of items in decoration and the act of calling on items in spells, but it is also often the same items which appear in both cases. The Sicklebill and Princess Stephanie birds, the White bird of paradise, red parrots, and numerous kinds of marsupial may all be called on in spells as well as used for ornaments. One spell cites nassa and green-snail shells specifically because of their shining quality.[21] In the past, when shells were scarcer, especially bright pearl shells were withdrawn from circulation and kept privately inside the owner's men's house. It was thought that their gleam would attract other pearl shells to them and the owner consequently be successful in *moka*.[22]

Putting on an item of decoration makes a direct association between the person and the article worn, and also imputes a transference of the item's ideal quality to the person himself – just as a spell imparts qualities to a bespelled person or object. At the same time a piece of decoration is thought to depend for its success on the actual recitation of spells (in some cases) and on prayers to ancestral ghosts (in all cases). If successful, it demonstrates the support of the ancestors, who hold fertility and prosperity within their power. Self-decoration thus involves spell-making, omen-taking, and the actual demonstration of success all in one.

THE MEANING OF DECORATIONS

Twice in the preceding section we have remarked that Hageners are not always explicit about why they follow ritual precautions when they are wearing decorations or about what the act of decorating means. But this need not be regarded as surprising. We may argue, in fact, that decorations transmit messages which are not exactly replicated in verbal behaviour or verbal explana-tions.[23] However, in attempting to discover what these messages are, we are necessarily dependent on verbal clues and exegesis from the Hageners themselves, supplemented by an analysis of the context in which decorations are worn and actual behaviour at festivals.

In discussing decorations with them, we found that Hageners made clear formulations as far as the appropriateness of a set of items to a particular type of occasion or to the status of a wearer was concerned. At this level of meaning, then, the cultural code is explicit and consciously applied. If one turns to the details of the items, on the other hand, asking perhaps why certain feathers, plants, or face-paints are used, responses vary. We have grouped these responses into three kinds, which fall along a continuum. At one end are very specific associations, at the other only general effects, or qualities, of decorations. However, the same general qualities are important also to the specific associations.

1. Some examples of specific associations have already appeared. We have noted that resin from the *kilt* tree is used in making a type of wig because of this tree's precise magical association with the quality of attractiveness. Again, eagle feathers are said to make the wearer successful in obtaining wealth, the rapacious, meat-hunting bird being compared with the wealth-seeking man (see above). Wearing Red bird plumes associates the dancer with the graceful movements of this bird of paradise when it is in display before females.

Few of the other feathers used have such direct associations. The *køi wal*, for example, important as it is, does not signify anything in these terms: 'It is just decoration,' Hageners say. Moreover the specific connotation that some items carry does not encompass their whole meaning, since they also contribute to a general effect which may or may not be present in the connotation itself.

2. Some items have associations similar to those mentioned in (1), but they are not as fully explicit. We have seen, for example, that when men are asked why they wear charcoal they say this is to disguise the wearer, or to make his body big, or that it indicates the presence of ancestral ghosts. To understand these comments we need to know more about what they refer to: why men should disguise themselves, what the effect of appearing big is, and why ancestral ghosts should come to men's faces – as we have attempted to explain.

3. Most of the articles worn, whether or not they have particular associations, contribute to what Hageners see as an overall effect. At the most general level people simply say that an item is 'good' or 'makes the skin good'. More particularly, the main effects stressed are an overall 'dark' or 'bright' appearance. Shells are put on because they are white or light-coloured and hence bright. The explanation for framing the cheeks with trailing feathers is that these make the face dark. Grasses and leaves can have the same result, and in addition they impart freshness. In context, either bright or dark effects can be 'good' (*kae*), although *colours* which produce these effects can in further contexts be described as 'bad' (*kit*): for example, black charcoal is good for disguising men's faces; while poison, which is also black and associated with secrecy, is described as bad because of its explicit connection with hostility. Clearly the interpretation of what 'good' means can be easily related to the overt aims of a particular display. But analysis is complicated by the fact that certain kinds of occasion are themselves considered bad. Thus warfare decorations can be 'good' in the sense of achieving the aim of terrifying enemies, but at the same time are 'bad' because warfare itself is a bad time and decorations for it should not be too splendid.

The connotations of brightness and darkness are also complicated, and we shall attempt to discuss them further in chapter seven. Here we note that while Hageners say that bright decorations belong to certain types of *moka* or cult

141

festival and dark decorations to others, and that in general all decorations should be bright in the sense of new-looking and not dull, they do not in so many words go further into precise colour associations. It is hard to tell, in fact, whether colours derive their meaning from, or impart their meaning to, the occasions when they are worn. Hageners imply, however, that achieving such a general effect as 'brightness' is an end in itself, and hence we are led to think that 'brightness' is a concept which carries meaning to them; our problem becomes why it should be a desired end.

To illustrate this problem of meaning further, we shall take up the wearing of plants as a part of self-decoration. Plants are worn particularly for the effects which they contribute to decoration, and their value is not mediated through any kind of economic value-in-exchange: unlike plumes, furs, shells, and weapons they are not in any way valuables in themselves.

THE SIGNIFICANCE OF PLANTS

In some cases plants can be used to convey quite explicit messages, usually connected with political relations between groups or with stages in a festival.

For example, *minimbø* (Highlands breadfruit) leaves may be placed on a special stake to which pigs have been tied, in order to convey the message that these pigs are actually to be eaten by the recipients and not passed on in further exchanges. The large breadfruit leaves are appropriate for carrying this message since they are used to cover layers of food in earth ovens. Similarly, *olka* (Celastraceae *Elaeodendron* sp.)[24] leaves may be held up by donors at the end of a ceremonial charge up and down a row of pigs to be given away at a *moka*. These leaves are a sign that they have no more pigs and the *moka* is over. Their use here is derived from the fact that after eating pig-meat men wipe their hands with these leaves, and the dancers are conveying the message that they 'wash their hands' of the *moka*.

Another example is that at the final stage of one sequence of ceremonial exchange the leaves of the liana *kuklnga* that have earlier decorated the dancers' faces are worn now in their bustles, to indicate that the time of decoration is over. The leaves are left behind on the ceremonial ground to wither and dry. Again, when a group makes *moka* its men may dance holding sweet potato leaves to remind its enemies of a previous taunt that the group had been killed off and 'harvested' like the leaves of a sweet potato garden, its ceremonial ground destroyed and made fit only for growing vegetables. Since the group is there to dance and display its numbers, the enemy's taunt is thus shown to be untrue. This usage resembles the 'netbags of greens' ceremony which we described in chapter three. Women participating in a similar ceremony, called *wur wur*,[25] may also wear *kuklumb* leaves. This action is a statment that their

Plate 80
A 'second-best' head-
dress made entirely of
leaves: ferns, Lauraceae,
Croton

husbands will soon make pearl shell *moka*, since *kuklumb* is considered magically to draw in shells to a man's house.

The same plant, *kuklumb*, women dancing *werl* may festoon around their necks, and these leaves are said to make the women's skin as beautiful and as glossy as they themselves are (Pl. 83, woman on right). The gloss of the leaves is at the same time likened to the sheen of pearl shells, and they are said to have a fragrant scent; and it is these two qualities which 'attract' shells. *Kuklumb* is used in rituals and called on in songs which accompany the building of new men's houses and it may be planted by men in special plots along with love-magic plants which are held to attract women.

Other leaves have similar powers of attraction, and may adorn houses where valuables are kept or cult houses which are said to 'shine'[26] (Col. pl. 29). These include the *kuklnga* (Euphorbiaceae *Claoxylon* sp.), *mara* (Lauraceae), *nggit nggrape* (Euphorbiaceae *Croton* sp.), the fern *nøng* (Cyatheaceae), and the bush *kengena* (Urticaceae *Elatostema* sp.), also employed in ritual to make feathers bright (Pls 80, 81).

While these are prominent in decorations, by no means all plants used in magic to obtain wealth are also used for ornaments. Thus, there is a kind of wild taro (Araceae *Colocasia* sp.)[27] which has the same magical properties as *kuklumb*, but it is not used for decorations because its leaf is flabby and wilts quickly. The *køpia* tree has red berries which attract birds, and is used to decorate houses, but not for personal adornment. It is called on in spells along with the *kilt* tree to attract wealth, but not chosen like the *kilt* for self-decoration. Conversely, many of the plants which are worn have no specific magical associations at all. As a category, however, they participate in a more general symbolism.

One of the qualities that we have seen admired in decoration is brightness. There are three components of meaning involved which we may touch on here, not all of which need be present for an item to be described as bright: (a) light colour, e.g. red, yellow, or white, as opposed to black; (b) a shining appearance, which both light- and dark-coloured items may possess, in the sense that both may be glossy; and (c) freshness or newness of appearance. The opposites of these three components of meaning are (a) dark colour, (b) dull appearance, (c) dry or 'dead' appearance.

The donning of leaves, ferns, and grasses is said particularly to impart component (c) to decorations. Plants are freshly picked for an occasion and are thus said to give a freshness to the whole attire. This quality of freshness is described as *kundil*,[28] a term which can mean 'new' and 'cool' as well as fresh and bright. Coolness is a quality which leaves share with running water, and both are further associated with fertility, in particular with male fertility.[29] The kind of moss which is wrapped round the *Wøp* cult stones when these are buried in

Plate 81
A Kuli wife (L)
includes *kuklnga* in her
armband

the earth is called *mul-koma* (*koma*=cool), and the action is also thought to increase fertility.

Certain leaves in addition denote components (a) and (b), and may therefore be described as *kurumukl*, white, or *keu*, shiny. They may be worn when the whole emphasis of decorations is on whiteness, as when the frothy inflorescence of *Miscanthus* cane is fluffed out over pig's tail aprons (Pl. 63). *Nggit nggrape* is popular for courting decorations since its bright yellow and green colours are held to attract girls (Pl. 11). *Mara* leaves, pale white in colour, are commonly pinned against black Enga wigs (Pl. 39) and worn along with black charcoal in warfare. Here the leaves are employed in a kind of complementary way to dark colours, as men may also use white face-paint. The majority of green plants, however, are spoken of as dark, i.e. dark- as opposed to light-coloured, and it is particularly these which have the attribute of being *kundil*. Indeed, if one asks why certain leaves are worn, one may be told either that they are *kurumukl, keu*, or that they are *kundil*. Nevertheless, plants that are said to have a glossy, gleaming appearance,[30] such as *kuklumb*, may also be described as *kundil*. *Kundil*, however, carries no close colour specifications. It primarily means 'fresh', and it is because of this quality that the plants are worn. This general quality is in turn sometimes connected with magical associations: the *kuklumb* leaves commented on as being *kundil* also have magical properties.

Since the quality of *kundil* is thus connected with ideas of fertility and magical power, it is not surprising that observers may be critical of dancers who have not bothered to complete their decorations by finding the proper plants and grasses to wear. There is also a further element involved, which links with our section on the involvement of ghosts in men's activities.

For big occasions it is especially from forest areas that plants are collected, and this activity is under the aegis of ghosts. Discovering fine specimens quickly is evidence of good luck and ancestral favour. Plants have to be the right ones, and men speak of the difficulty with which they obtain them. Finding the best types of plants is more important for the bigger occasions, whereas for second-best decoration, e.g. courting parties, there are recognised substitutes, usually ones growing near to settlement places. The most highly valued plants tend to be those which are thought to remain fresh for the longest time after they are picked and thus to show the power of freshness most clearly; and to be ones which are important in magic.

Elsewhere[31] we have analysed the contrast which Hageners make between 'wild' and 'domestic' things and the association which they see between wild things and strength or power. The best plant decorations, then, are not only *kundil*, but come from places (primarily the forest) which are wild and strong.

It is true that two of the shrubs picked for ornaments may be planted

Plate 82
Leaves casually tucked
into the belt for informal
decoration

(*kuklumb* and *nggit nggrape*) although several other important ones are not;[32] and Hagen men also bring back forest-tree seedlings to plant at their ceremonial grounds. But forest trees are planted in this way precisely because of their origin, and hence their qualities of wild strength. It is not that the trees become truly domesticated by the act of planting but that the ceremonial grounds become allied to the wild domain.[33] The major edible crops grown in gardens – tubers and green vegetables[34] – do not contribute to decorations at all (except in special usages, as we have mentioned earlier); and this contrast between edible plants and the non-edible ones[35] used for decoration parallels the contrast between private, secular garden areas and public ceremonial grounds associated with ancestor spirits.

Cordylines fall into a different category from those forest plants which we have been discussing and which are spoken of as especially *kundil*. At least fourteen kinds of plants are worn by both sexes at festivals and these include all of the important forest plant decorations except for *mara* and *nøng*, which appear to be specific to men (although this is not the subject of an explicit rule). This sharing of forest plants for decoration seems to equate the sexes, as does the general fact of wearing feathers of forest birds (including *ketepa*, King of Saxony, which is said to have stolen its long crests, valued for ornaments, from a grass-land bird and made off with these into the deep forests from which it no longer ventures); whereas they are distinguished, as we have seen, by face-paint and by colour emphases. Men sometimes explicitly say that in decorating women become like men, and the wearing of these plants corroborates this kind of statement.

Cordylines, however, differentiate males from females (as also do aprons). The types that men wear most commonly, both everyday and for dancing, are dark green in colour and planted only by men (Pl. 76). They mark the boundaries of a person's gardens and settlements, fringe ceremonial grounds (for they are associated with ancestors and are the divination-substance[36] of certain tribes), and are said to indicate the area of human habitation to wild bush-spirits.

Women wear these green cordylines only in mourning. Otherwise, for courting parties, *moka* dances (and also sometimes when they are menstruating) they don coloured ones: dark red or crimson, variegated red and yellow, and yellow and green (Col. pl. 25). These are all types which are planted not at the edges of gardens but to mark internal boundaries between the private plots of women, or simply planted in clumps within garden areas. They seem to be worn only by women (Pls 79, 83). On the occasions when men are dancing *mør* and when women are present, the men may add a variety of wild sprigs from forest plants to their 'domestic' cordyline bustles (Pl. 84), whereas

148

Plate 83
Women's *werl* cordylines
are crinkled to add to
their glitter

Plate 84
Forest shrub, fern and
pine leaves in men's
bustles

women do not do so, but instead wear a profusion of crinkled red cordylines. It is true that on some occasions or when wearing pig's tail aprons men may don coloured cordylines that are bright and planted in garden areas. But the actual types of cordyline they choose are on the whole named differently from those which women put on, and the style with which they are worn is different also. Only boys, whose red-painted faces equate them with females, also wear women's cordylines.

Cordylines, then, have a different function from the wild forest plants, and they are not especially spoken of as *kundil*.

One plant also seems peculiar to men. This is the white *mara*, worn specifically for warfare as well as for cults and festivals. It is rarely worn by women but is one of the commonest items of male decoration (e.g. Pls 49, 50).

Men and women alike, then, may wear about their head and arms similar fresh leaves and wild plants. They remain explicitly contrasted by their aprons and cordylines, as well as by their face-paint.

In this final section of the chapter we have examined specific magical qualities of plants and also their general effect of freshness. We have seen how this attribute relates to the opposition between dark and bright decoration effects, and pointed out that it is a quality which is claimed by both sexes (whereas cordylines differentiate them). In the next chapter we shall examine the dark/bright opposition and the male/female opposition further.

CHAPTER SEVEN

The connotations of colour

We have often referred to the two attributes of decorations which Hageners emphasise: the bright quality of certain shells, plumes, furs, and paints, and the dark quality of charcoal, Enga wigs, men's long aprons, and the *køi wal* head-dress; and we discussed how plants, as things which are 'fresh' (*kundil*) can contribute further to either quality in a person's set of decorations.

Both qualities, when exhibited in decorations for festivals and cults, are admired. Dark ornaments disguise their wearer, making it hard for spectators to recognise him, and they are also said to increase the wearer's appearance of size and strength. Bright decorations, if applied in profusion, can also dis-guise, but that is not their chief aim. What is emphasised about them is that they attract pigs, valuables, and the opposite sex. Bright colours are also a demonstration of fertility, shown in success at rearing pigs, when worn by married women performing the *werl* dance, by men when they dance in pig's tail aprons, and by men again in the Female Spirit cult. But there are complica-tions in the analysis of brightness, as we have suggested at the end of the last chapter; and there are ambiguities in the evaluation of the two attributes also, which in this chapter we attempt to elucidate.

We have seen that there is an overall concern that feathers should be bright, in the sense of new-looking or shining, as opposed to dull. To this end, men protect their feathers from menstruating women, abstain from intercourse while decorating themselves or making special wigs, and in the past performed specific rituals over the feathers themselves. This concern applies to all feathers, including those that are considered at the same time to be relatively dark, such as *kɸi wal*.[1] We have to distinguish two levels of meaning for the term bright: at the highest level it refers to a new, glossy, or shining appearance; whereas at a lower level it refers specifically to things which are light in colour and therefore shining by contrast with things which are dark in colour. Moreover, as we shall argue later, there is a further level at which white is to some extent contrasted with other light colours such as red, yellow, and blue. If we wished to represent this logically, we could do so as follows:

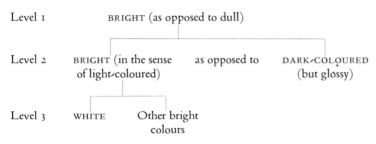

Level 1   BRIGHT (as opposed to dull)

Level 2   BRIGHT (in the sense   as opposed to   DARK-COLOURED
           of light-coloured)   (but glossy)

Level 3   WHITE   Other bright
                    colours

It should be noted that there are certain dark items in decoration, for example charcoal and Enga wigs when these are worn without grease, which one does not hear described as bright at all; instead, their contrast with bright things at level 2 is what receives emphasis. Further, at this level, although dark decorations are described as good, bright ones seem to evoke an even more enthusiastic response. At this level also, bright decorations seem to be particularly appropriate to women, and certainly women choose brighter face-colours than men. Darker, restrained decorations are the ones appropriate to men, except when their specific aim is to attract women. Significantly, men themselves sometimes agree that women's more profuse and bright decorations are better than theirs, and that bright colours painted on cheeks are the best designs of all.[2] Yet a base of charcoal is specific to males on most occasions. It is surprising, in fact, to hear Hagen men saying that any decorations which are characteristic of women can be better than those particular to themselves, for one of the salient emphases in self-decoration among them is the aggrandisement of male rather than female strength. The groups which hold displays are corporate bodies of males, and the occasions for display are frequently political exchanges or warfare between these groups. Participation in cult rituals, if not in dancing, is restricted to men, and only men sacrifice and pray to clan ancestors to achieve success in these activities. Women have no elaborate festivals of their own. When they dance, it is as participants in events controlled by men. Thus it is that decorating is thought by the Hageners to be somehow more appropriate to men than to women. Moreover, we have seen how women's menstrual

153

powers are thought to threaten men's health, which is on display at festivals. Hence it is surprising that despite all this men still say that female decorations can be better in some respects than theirs.

The paradox is increased by parallel statements which informants make, that when women decorate elaborately they become like men ('turn into men', *wuᵉ raremen*), and that hence their decorations are dark and good like those of men. People may even say that the women's own natal ancestors come to their faces and help to make them dark, as they do in the case of men. Clearly, these statements are not consistent with those of informants who urge that, in decorating, females become brighter and hence better than males. In the one version women are merged with men; in the other they are opposed. And in the first case, a dark appearance is said to be pre-eminently good; whereas in the second this value is claimed for bright decorations.

Again, in warfare decorations darkness is emphasised, and the black charcoal which is rubbed over the fighters' bodies is said to make them impressive; yet the total set of decorations is also said to be bad by comparison with those for festivals. Hageners are quite explicit about this. They state that warfare is bad, because it carries with it the possibility of death, and so bad decorations are appropriate for it. Hence only second-best plumes, or plumes in second-rate, dull condition were chosen for it.

Moreover the same was suggested by one informant of the charcoal employed to disguise the warrior. 'At the time of fighting men do not put on good face-paint or good grease, they wear charcoal only [*ndip tap mint*], and they do not cover their faces with all the good little pieces of ornament which are worn at the time of festival dances. The decoration for warfare is bad [*moke kit*].' The contrast here is between a profusion of decorations carefully applied to the face, and charcoal used to cover not only the face but the whole body as well; and between the use of various face-paints and the adornment of the body with grease for dances, and the absence of these items in warfare decorations. The total effect in the latter case is said to be bad (*kit*). When informants are not contrasting warfare and dance decorations with each other, they may speak of the charcoal in a more positive way: 'Warriors put charcoal all over their skin, so that people will think a big-man is coming, and if they are killed people will be sorry too, for they will say that a big-man with beautiful decorations has died. They put charcoal on also to prevent their enemies from recognising them: the charcoal disguises them and makes them bigger.'

It is clear, then, that levels of evaluation are involved here. Charcoal is good for the purpose of making wearers impressive and disguising them; but it may be evaluated as bad in the context of warfare simply because warfare itself is bad. Nor is it just that charcoal is bad in itself: it is the mode of application

TABLE 4: *Melpa terms for bright and dark colour effects in decorations*[1]

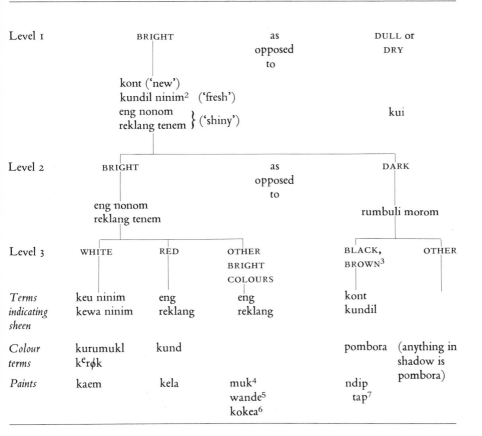

Level 1   BRIGHT   as   DULL or
                             opposed   DRY
                               to

           kont ('new')
           kundil ninim[2] ('fresh')
           eng nonom   ⎱   kui
           reklang tenem ⎰ ('shiny')

Level 2   BRIGHT   as   DARK
                             opposed
                               to

           eng nonom   rumbuli morom
           reklang tenem

Level 3   WHITE   RED   OTHER   BLACK,   OTHER
                               BRIGHT   BROWN[3]
                               COLOURS

Terms   keu ninim   eng   eng   kont
indicating kewa ninim reklang reklang   kundil
sheen

Colour   kurumukl   kund   pombora (anything in
terms   kᵉrøk   shadow is
                                                       pombora)
Paints   kaem   kela   muk[4]   ndip
                                wande[5]   tap[7]
                                kokea[6]

Notes
1. This table is not designed to show the complete range of meanings for the terms given in it, but some of the relationships between the terms relevant to decoration effects.
2. *Ninim, nonom, tenem, morom* are all existential verb forms here. Thus *kundil ninim*, 'it is fresh'. There are further terms which in some contexts may carry the general meaning of 'gleaming'. For example, *nggri tinim* can be used of the bright yellow streaks found in one type of cordyline: they are compared to flames which 'glow'.
3. 'Brown' cassowary plumes, however, are classed as red, *kund*.
4, 5, 6. These are terms for earth paints: light blue, orange, and yellow respectively. The table does not include terms for coloured clays and muds which are used exclusively as a sign of mourning or protest, indicating a mental upset, and are not employed for decoration at all. Concomitantly, they do not fall under the rubric 'bright'. Examples are: *kentilpantel* (dark orange to greeny-yellow), *kengᵉkla wangkᵉkla* (brown to yellow), *teringi* (black mud), and *nggoa* (soot mixed with grease).
7. Charcoal. Also known as *øruma* (specifically, charcoal prepared with pig-fat).

A. WHITE	1. Performers in the Female Spirit cult wear white feathers and head⁄nets, are told by ritual experts not to use poison because this is black and associated with hostility. The Spirit herself is said to have white, shining cobwebs round her head which the dancers' head⁄nets imitate.
	2. White decorations are worn with pig's tail aprons to show that the wearers are strong and have 'grease', eat pig⁄fat. The gleam of grease on the skin also indicates health.
	3. The white gleam of shells is said magically to attract further shells to the wearers of decorations.
	4. The gleam of bright (including white) ornaments is said to terrify enemies in warfare.
B. RED AND OTHER BRIGHT COLOURS	1. Women like bright colours, especially red, for their face⁄paint, and particularly for *werl* dancing.
	2. Men put on wigs reddened with ochre and painted with other bright colours in order to attract girls to themselves at *ware* dances.
	3. Red ochre is a magical substance, said to attract shells and valuables.
	4. Red ochre paint is worn in warfare after men have completed an act of revenge⁄taking. It signifies that they feel good.
	5. Sometimes red paint when worn by men is said to be bad, because it is too transparent and allows dancers to be recognised. Again, Red plumes are sometimes spoken of as bad by comparison with the dark *køi wal*.
C. BLACK	1. Poison, the means of covert hostility between groups, is spoken of and identified in autopsies as a black substance.
	2. Charcoaling the body makes men look bigger and hence more frightening when they are going out to fight in warfare.
	3. Charcoaling the face also makes male dancers imposing at a festival, and disguises them so that they cannot be easily recognised. For this reason, men prefer to wear a charcoal base to their face⁄paint, especially along with *køi wal* and Enga wigs.
	4. Darkness as an overall effect of decorations is said to be good and is an ideal for men. It implies that ancestral ghosts have come to support the men (in their dancing, in fighting).

that is important. The implication is that decorations applied without pains⁄taking care and which lack a balance between bright and dark elements are bad by comparison with those worn at dances. Meanings that charcoal can carry may be similar in both warfare and festivals; it is the total set of decorations and the total context in which they are displayed that receive evaluation.

Meaning, as well as evaluation, of decorations may, however, depend at

TABLE 6: *Summary of decorations worn on different occasions*

		Men's decorations	Women's decorations (werl)
CULTS	Female Spirit	Emphasis on white (+red) = bright	Women do not dance
	Wøp Spirit	Emphasis on dark (+bright)	Bright decorations with red faces
EXCHANGE	Large gifts between opposed groups	Emphasis on dark (+bright)	Bright decorations with red faces, profusion makes them also look 'dark'
	Smaller-scale, where less opposition	Brighter feathers than in large gifts	Women do not dance*
	Pig-killing festivals	Bright red or other bright-coloured wigs; or bright feathers	Women join in the line in bright decorations; or do not dance
	Pig-moka (with pig's tail aprons)	Emphasis on white (+red) = bright	Women do not dance* (on one occasion they decorated and ran up and down the line of pigs, but did not dance)
WARFARE	Major warfare	Emphasis on dark (+bright)	Women do not take part
	Minor warfare	No decorations	Women do not take part

* Girls may dance as clan sisters, when they follow men's decorations and dance with them, but have brighter faces and sometimes brighter feathers.

least partly on context. Thus, in the *ware* dance brightly coloured wigs were worn to attract women; in warfare bright plumes and shells were put on to terrify male enemies. The function of bright colour seems to be quite different in the two cases. But there may also be a linkage between the two functions, as statements on the reaction of spectators to large, bright wigs suggest: women are first terrified and then attracted by them. For the women here fear and attrac-tion are perhaps not incompatible, and the same display can produce both reactions; whereas in the context of warfare the same colours when displayed before other males might produce only the first reaction of the two. The elements of shock and surprise, however, occur in both contexts.

In this case, the meaning given to bright decorations varies with the context in which they are worn; in the case of charcoal, the meanings may be similar in two situations, but the situations themselves give rise to different evaluations. We also suggest that where colours have different implications in separate contexts then the meaning relevant in one context can be covertly transferred to, or can intrude into, other contexts; and that it is this process of intrusion which gives an ambiguity to the evaluation of colours.

Before we attempt to illustrate this last proposition further, we shall summarise some of the facts on which we are constructing our ideas (Tables 4, 5, 6).

It can be seen that our breakdown of the category 'bright' into white+red+ other bright colours, in opposition to black, is similar to Turner's identification of a basic colour triad, consisting of white, red, and black.[3] But there are also differences in our scheme. In the first place we have distinguished between two levels of meaning for brightness, such that dark-coloured things (e.g. *køi wal* head-dresses), if they are glossy (*eng nonom*) and new-looking (*kont*, *kundil*), can be described as bright at level 1, although they are also opposed to bright (i.e. light-coloured) things at level 2. Second, whether an item of decoration is termed dark or not is a matter of overall effect, not simply of colour. Thus, *køi wal* contains red plumage and Saxony feathers which are certainly light in colour (*kund*, *kurumukl*), but it also includes much dark-blue plumage, and when worn with an Enga wig it has a relatively dark overall appearance (*rumbuli*). Third, 'bright' includes yellow and light blue as well as white and red, and 'dark' includes anything in shadow or which contributes to an overshadowing effect, as well as black. Finally, even if we were to exclude the other colours and were to say that this system is fundamentally triadic, consisting of white, red, and black, it would still remain the case that these elements are not contrasted triadically. Instead white+red may be summed as 'bright' and contrasted with 'dark'; or white+black may be summed as 'male' and contrasted with red as 'female'. The contrasts involved are always dyadic.[4] Moreover, men can at times specifically arrogate to themselves the use of red and other bright colours in order to increase their sexual attractiveness; and in this context the sexes are not differentiated in terms of colour preferences, for women use bright colours to make themselves attractive, too, but in terms of their hair: the men's large wigs unambiguously identify them as male.

Abstracting from the material in our tables, we propose the following overall associations:

RED	WHITE	BLACK
Brightness: fertility, attractiveness		Darkness: disguise, aggressiveness
Female (+male) associations	Predominantly male associations	Male associations

158

Colour	Overt association	Latent association
Dark decorations (black)	increase size; disguise identity; show presence of ghosts	male aggressiveness and solidarity
Bright decorations (white) including oil and grease	make body look healthy; frighten enemies; attract valuables; attract opposite sex	male fertility and group continuity (semen)
Bright decorations (red and other bright colours) including red paint	attract valuables; attract opposite sex	male attractiveness; female attractiveness and fertility; links of friendship between groups, i.e. ties through women (blood)

Men are thus associated, in different contexts, both with dark and with bright decorations; women only with bright ones. We detect, in fact, a polarisation, in which red comes to be predominantly associated with females, white and black with males. This polarisation is expressed most clearly in the face-paint worn by the two sexes.

However, we have also seen that the item of decoration which makes men most sexually attractive is precisely the *kilt* wig, which is wholly red, and is associated both with the *kilt* tree and with the magical powers of red ochre, which attracts valuables and pigs as well as women. This dual association of red with both men and women prompts us to generalise further and to suggest that red represents the flow of friendly and positive communication between groups and between men and women as sexual partners. It is wealth and women together. Hageners speak of interpersonal kin ties through women as 'blood' ties, and of pearl shells, important wealth items, as having a ruddy colour (*kund*) as well as a sheen (*reklang*). The shells are also freshly decorated with red ochre whenever they are used for a payment between groups, and not to do so is to run the risk of death (the opposite of life and fertility).

We must emphasise, then, that there is no *exclusive* sex-linkage of the colour red in Hagen, although black is unequivocally associated with men. As Turner has said for Ndembu:[5] 'Colour symbolism is not consistently sex-linked, although red and white may be situationally specified to represent the opposition of the sexes.'

One prominent situation in which we have identified such a specification is in the dancing for a major pig-moka. Similarly, the bright/dark opposition is relevant in differentiating men's dress for important exchange festivals from that for less important ones. Women's decorations for exchange festivals more constantly stress bright colours and a profusion of items than do men's, and the colour red is a noticeable part of this emphasis. Men's decorations are more explicitly stated to be an amalgam of dark and bright things, but their overall emphasis to be dark. Using the associations which we have abstracted earlier from what Hageners themselves say, we argue that dark elements in decorations imply aggressiveness, bright ones friendship.[6]

The political attitude of men towards groups with whom they conduct exchanges is itself an amalgam of aggressiveness and friendship, and although men do not formulate this in abstract terms it is evident from their speeches at festivals that they themselves play on this point, sometimes stressing common interests, sometimes reviving old disagreements between their own groups and others. This complex of attitudes is in turn weighted differently in minor and major festivals. At minor festivals where the exchanges are internal to a tribe or between close allies, prestige is not so much at stake and aggressiveness is less important. At major festivals it becomes more important, for these involve groups which are in a more intensely competitive relationship. We argue, then, that it is appropriate that men wear brighter decorations for minor festivals, darker ones for major occasions. Women, by contrast, wear very bright decorations at the major festivals themselves. It is specifically the function of women to link groups in friendly relations through inter-clan marriages, and women are not usually responsible for representing inter-clan opposition as men are. This function, again, is not expressed by Hageners as a part of a sociological analysis of their own society, but it is stated clearly in such idioms as 'we exchange women, we are friends', or 'there is a marriage (or a tie of blood) between us, we see a road (i.e. we can have exchange relations)'. If, then, women are the prime means whereby inter-group friendship is activated, it is fitting that they should stress brightness (especially redness) in their decorations.

At the same time we have seen that informants also argue that in a sense the women who decorate themselves profusely and dance *werl* at pig-moka festivals are dark like men. We interpret this as referring not to inter-group relations but to the relationship between husband and wife. This stress on parallelism in men's and women's decorations points to the close co-operation of the sexes in rearing pigs, and to an identification of the women's interests with those of their husband's clan; and it actually suppresses what is an obvious sexual dimorphism, recognised in other statements that women's decorations are much brighter than men's.

The same theme of interdependence between the sexes appears in the two main religious cults.

In the Female Spirit cult there is a strong emphasis on white decorations (white head-net, White bird plumes, sticks of fluffy white eagle feathers) and a secondary one on red (Red plumes, red cordylines in the rear covering). Women may not dance at or otherwise take part in the cult. The fact that females are excluded would fit with the stress on white decorations, if these, as we have asserted, are especially associated with men. But why may not women take part? We can suggest two reasons: the Female Spirit is pure, non-menstrual, unlike human females, and if women joined in the cult they might pollute the men. Secondly, by excluding women the men are asserting that their own male fertility is sufficient to perpetuate the clan. Then why is the Spirit regarded as female at all? The association of red ochre with attraction and fertility on the one hand and women on the other reveals that in other contexts Hageners are quite aware of the physical importance of women in perpetuating their groups and that groups cannot perpetuate themselves unless they also establish links between each other. We suggest that this is given covert recognition in the fact that the Spirit is female. She is like a woman in that she is female and also links groups together (by the passage of the cult from one clan to another); but she is like a male also, in that she does not bear children and is particularly associated with the colour white. The men's white decorations reflect her male qualities; their secondary emphasis on red implies a recognition of the importance of human females. Overall the decorations are bright, and quite different from those appropriate to important *moka* festivals.

As we remarked in chapter four, the *Wøp* cult ought, in a sense, to follow this pattern also, and it is possible that at some performances of it the decorations *have* been similarly bright. But the difference between the two cults is that in the *Wøp* the interdependence of the sexes is recognised quite openly. Although women are excluded from the central rituals of the cult itself, which are assertions or symbols of male fertility and male clan unity, they may join in the final dancing. We suggest that women's actual participation as dancers brings a further factor into play: the need to differentiate the sexes. In the performance which we saw differentiation was achieved by the adoption of decorations appropriate to pig-moka when women are dancing *werl*. The sexes were thus separated, but at the same time linked to each other, just as we have seen for the case of pig-moka festivals themselves; and this is appropriate for a cult celebrating the interdependence of the sexes.

We thus have three contexts in which colour contrasts are linked with contrasts between males and females. In the Female cult women may not dance, and men are able to arrogate to themselves both white and red colours, with emphasis on the former. In the two other contexts (pig-moka and *Wøp* cult) both men and women dance. Women wear bright red face-paint and a profusion of bright feathers and shells, both red and white, while men have darker colours and large black wigs. The message here seems to be that the sexes are interdependent but each has a separate contribution to make towards fertility; whereas in the Female Spirit cult men go further towards claiming that they alone are responsible for fertility.

We are now in a position to return to the paradox which we outlined at the beginning of this chapter: that although Hagen men regard themselves in general as superior to women, they sometimes say that the bright decorations women wear for *werl* dancing are better than men's darker ones. We can interpret this as a kind of covert moral evaluation of relations between groups. Bright, especially red, decorations stand for positive communication between groups, dark ones for aggressiveness and opposition. What the men are saying is something which appears to conflict with their dominant political ideology of clan strength: that friendship is better than aggressiveness. In fact, however, there is no absolute contradiction here, for it is by strength, by powers of attraction, that groups draw each other into networks of friendship.

It is important to note, also, that the evaluations of colours are ambivalent. We have already made some mention of black. Although red is usually regarded as good, attractive, and so on, it is sometimes spoken of by men as bad (*kit*), especially when they speak of wearing it themselves in the form of face-paint (cf. Table 5, B5). To explain this ambivalence, we suggest that in the context of decorations the meaning which the colour red has in other contexts becomes *suppressed*, but that, in the manner we hypothesised earlier, it nevertheless *intrudes* into decoration contexts.

The most obvious association, to us, between the colour red and physical things is that between redness and blood. Yet, though Hageners recognise this association, it is not one to which they draw attention in discussing the importance of red things in decoration. This, we suggest, is because blood, like the blood ties which link groups, is regarded ambivalently.[7]

Men marry women of other clans. It is particularly blood which a mother contributes to the body of her child, and this blood is the blood of her own natal clan. The father of the child provides the initial grease (*kopong*, i.e. semen), which, when mixed with blood, causes conception. Both blood and grease are thus important agents of fertility. But women's menstrual blood, which is considered to be similar to the blood which with semen forms a 'packet' in a mother's womb, is dangerous to men. It is, in fact, antithetical to men's 'grease'. Should a man ingest it, either through his penis during intercourse, or in his food, his skin would lose its grease and become dry and his body emaciated. Even if a woman is not menstruating, it is thought that traces of menstrual blood may adhere to her genitals, so that there is always a risk of pollution during

162

sexual contact. Loss of semen in intercourse itself can make a man's skin dry and weaken him. We have described earlier the taboos that result from these notions: the prohibitions against intercourse when men are decorating, or against menstruating women participating in dances or handling feathers, lest the ornaments turn dull and the decorating oil dry up.

Female blood may thus be either good or bad: good in that it makes children grow, bad when it appears in menstrual form, for then it is inimical to the grease of grown men.

The same is true of male semen. Semen helps to create children, and is a manifestation of male vitality and health; but it is inimical to mother's milk, and for this reason a man should not have intercourse with his wife while she has a child whom she is suckling. If he did so his semen would pollute the milk in her breasts, which the child would ingest; and it would waste away and die. We cannot simply argue, then, that semen is regarded as pure and menstrual blood as polluting. Each can be polluting, in particular contexts.[8]

In the context of decorations these ambivalent values of semen and blood are never overtly introduced.[9] Oil and grease fall into the same general category as semen (*kopong*), and seem to be partially equated with it, since semen is thought of as like the 'grease' which makes men's skin appear healthy, and decorating oils also make the skin look good. But the decorating oils are never explicitly stated to be like semen, and are given no harmful powers. Similarly, red ochre paint is never said to resemble blood, although blood is said to be red (*kund*) like it. In decoration, it is positive values that are accorded these two colours: both stand for productiveness, health, and attractiveness. We notice only that men sometimes speak of Red plumes or red paint as bad things (*mel kundi, mel kit*; *mel kit*, 'bad thing', is also the regular term for female or male genitals); and we suggest that this evaluation results from the intrusion of a suppressed association with blood.

In other contexts, the ambiguity of the colour red is clearly revealed. In spells, for example, red lakes (*nu kund*) are dangerous whereas dark ones (*nu pombora*) are not; the red lakes devour men, but they also give forth herds of pigs. They may be called upon in spells to yield up valuables too. Again, in customary belief there are wild spirits which haunt woodland places: the red ones are often harmful, while the black ones are not. In mythology one finds as a recurrent element that a man has two wives, one dark (*pombora*) the other light-coloured (*kund*) in skin.[10] The latter is revealed in the stories to be a hostile spirit, who tries to kill either her co-wife or her husband. Thus, although an opposition between things which are 'red' (*kund*) and things which are 'black' (*pombora*) appears in spells, folklore, and mythology as well as in decoration, the opposition is not given the same value in the case of decoration. In fact, here the values

163

seem to be reversed, for we have argued that black charcoal signifies aggressive-ness (i.e. danger) whereas red paint stands for attractiveness and friendship.

The values are not, however, entirely contradictory, as one of the examples we have mentioned, that of the red and black wild spirits, shows. People some-times say that the black (*pombora*) wild spirits look after men's pigs in the bush and also protect men against the attacks of the red (*kund*) ones. Their function here is analogous to that of the ancestors, who protect men in battle and help them in their dancing; and the sign of the ancestors' presence also is that the men 'look dark' (*pombora*). In fact, we might argue that black signifies outward-looking aggressiveness with its corollary of inward-looking support and protec-tion. An outward show of hostility may also be a demonstration of internal solidarity. Friendship between men of different clans, on the other hand, is friendship towards outsiders and carries a latent corollary of hostility within the clan itself, since outward links may weaken internal ones. It is appropriate, then, that both black and red can stand for danger and friendship, in the case of decorations directed towards outsiders, and in the context of folk-lore directed towards men who are threatened from outside. If red means friendship towards outsiders, its opposite black means hostility; if red means danger to internal protection and solidarity, black carries an affirmation of these.

A parallel ambiguity appears within the category of things which are white. We have already remarked on the different connotations of bright (including white) ornaments in decoration for warfare and decoration for festivals, which are discussed again below. We can add to this the example of white clay or lime (*kaem*).

Men say that the clay resembles white pig-fat and that is why it is worn on the legs and on pig's tail aprons for pig-*moka* festivals. It is like grease, and in this sense stands for health and attractiveness. The same meaning explains why the clay is rubbed on sick pigs to make them healthy. But men also say that white clay is like ashes, and ashes have both 'good' and 'bad' connotations. On the one hand ashes are compared to grease, and they, too, can be rubbed over pigs' backs to bring them back to health. On the other hand, in certain contexts, it is not the white colour of ashes and *kaem* which are stressed, but their dryness when applied to the skin, and this dryness is actually the antithesis of grease: it connotes ill-health, poor skin condition, and mourning, and this explains why, as we describe later, both white clay and ashes are worn at funerals. We can represent the situation diagrammatically:

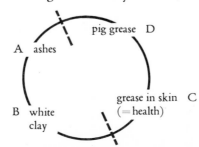

Colour plate 1
A crowd fills the dancing ground, pressing to within a spear's length of the performers. Many of the male visitors have spears themselves; wives carry bamboo water vessels to refresh their husbands in the dancing line

Colour plate 2
The brightness of pearl shells: a prestation accompanying a Female Spirit Cult performance. Freshly ochred boards enhance the desired ruddy colour in the shells

Colour plate 3
Weapons in hand, aprons kilted up, dancers charge down the double line of pearl shells, their last proud and aggressive gesture before the gift is handed over. On large occasions head-dresses have to be removed at this stage for fear of the crush

Colour plate 4
Donors at a Kuli festival make their *kanan*-dance entry, distinguished by feather plaques above the black Enga-style wigs

Colour plate 5
Drummers clear a space in front of the dancers (Northern Melpa festival). The feather plaques, horned wigs, and long net aprons have a 'dark' effect, and faces are blackened in accord with this

Colour plate 6
As well as pearl shell crescents, mounted shell valuables may be worn, here by Ndika men dancing *mør*

Colour plate 7
Feather plaque (*kǿi wal*). Set against the russet
fan of the Red bird of paradise, crown plumes
from the King of Saxony divide up a panel,
here coloured with tiny feathers from parrots,
lorikeets, water fowl, and a white-feathered owl

Colour plate 8
Oil is wiped over the shoulders, back, and chest
and on the dancer's bustle. This is at a practice:
he is fully painted, but wears only a single
White bird of paradise spray

Colour plate 9
The *kɸi wal* set: feather plaque flanked by sticks of the Blue bird, topped with Saxony streamers. A pearl shell crescent hangs over this important man's exchange tally

Colour plate 10
A young Ndika dancer (donor). In the same way as white and red paint contrasts with the charcoaled cheeks and beard, white Lauraceae leaves and a shell roundel show up his dark wig

Colour plate 11
Patterns painted on the face are named: a
'bending branch' under the eyes, 'forked insect's
tail' over the bridge of the nose, 'pig's tusk'
across the cheeks. The dots bordering the cheek
design can also give it the appellation 'spear
barbs'

Colour plate 12
Red bird plumes spurt from eagle and *kumin*
feathers, and the glossy ruff of the Superb bird of
paradise, an arrangement classified as a 'bright'
one

Colour plate 13
As an alternative to the plaque, Ndika donors wear multiple Red bird plumes and white cockatoo feathers, in one case along with Blue bird sticks

Colour plate 14
A helper at a Northern Melpa dance, an idiosyncratic touch in his fan from the Goura pigeon. Leaves festoon his face – Lauraceae and orchid at the ears, ferns and the liana *kuklnga* dripping from the beard

Colour plate 15
The velvet capes and breast shields of three
Superb birds of paradise shine like the dancer's
own hair and skin, which glisten with grease.
Blackened ear pendants made from nicked-out
kumin feathers emphasise the 'dark' aspect of his
decorations, the paint and white roundel complement this with 'brightness'

Colour plate 16
Men dancing with a young sister. She is dressed
for display as they are, but differentiated from
them: a yellow reed apron and red cordylines
where the men have long 'dark' net aprons,
eagle plumage where they wear *kɨi wal* plaques,
a red ochred face instead of their charcoaled ones

Colour plate 17
Male dancers at a Kuli festival with a young girl in their midst – the colour in the men's faces is minimal

Colour plate 18
Little girls parade at the end of a line of women

Colour plate 19
Wives of Kuli men, their hands raised in drum beat, perform *werl* to celebrate their own part in a prestation of pigs

Colour plate 20
The wives of men 'helping' a dance have combinations of feathers different from those of the donors' wives, but the same brilliant face-paint

Colour plate 23
The profuse array of a woman's plumage (Kuli, donor's wife)

Colour plate 24
A woman's decorations reflect the affluence and good connections of her husband, and it is probably her husband's exchange tally that this dancer is wearing. The wine-red cordylines in her armband are of a kind that have the power to draw in wealth by their attractiveness

Colour plate 25
Young girls decorated with oil and beads, faces painted, attending a festival where they later took part in an informal *mørli* dance. Unlike formal participants, they wear no feathers

Colour plate 26
As they dance women present not only their faces but their backs to spectators. One wears a mounted pearl shell over her crimped and variegated cordylines, a gift for her own kinsmen as a sign of her ties with them

Colour plate 29
The 'shining' cult house *(Wøp)*. Fresh ferns to be used in the cult are carried through the entrance of the enclosure which is adorned with 'bright' *mara* and *kundumb* leaves

Colour plate 30
Women mourners (foreground), covered in white clay and ashes, round a newly arrived clan sister who has smeared herself with orange mud

Colour plate 31
A *peng koem* wig. Resin,
which can be seen at the
unpainted rim of the dome,
stiffens the structure of hair
and provides a hard base
for the paint – here executed
in a pattern called 'swiftlet's
wings'. The stripes may also
be called by the same term
as a face design, *kerua*

In some contexts we find that A, B, C, and D are all equated; in others that B, C, and D or A, C, and D are equated. In these contexts A and B are the signifiers, the symbols that stand for C and D. But in other situations we find that A and C are opposites. Thus a big-man is described as *kopong iti wu^e*, 'a man who makes grease' (i.e. health and wealth)[11] and contrasted with a man of low status who is *korpa kik wu^e*, 'a poor ashes man'.[12] And in funerals A and B are equated in contrast again with C. (We also note that the dryness of *kaem* can be put to positive ritual use in other situations: for example, it is smeared over the belly of a woman suffering from excessive menstrual flow.[13] The clay's dry quality is supposed magically to stop the flow of blood. Similarly, it is used to cure pigs of dysentery.)

We thus have the paradoxical situation that whereas in some contexts white clay connotes grease and health, in others it connotes precisely the opposite: dryness and physical debility, associated with the mental state of mourning. In the latter situation its white colour may not be relevant at all, and hence we cannot draw a conclusion from these examples that white itself can directly stand for both health and ill-health. Instead we have to consider further qualities of the substance we are concerned with, to see whether it is their whiteness which is important in all the contexts or not.

Our later discussion of mourning will indicate, as is partly the case for charcoal, that it is the manner in which white clay is applied that is a crucial component of its meaning. The fact that it is white (*kurumukl*) does not seem to have any specific message in the context of mourning, as we have suggested that it does in decoration; nevertheless, this whiteness is an attribute of *kaem* which links it to grease on the one hand and to ashes on the other.

In so far as we maintain, then, that there are ambiguities in the attributes of white clay, the colours red and black seem analogous. For red the parallel is clear. Red is the colour of red ochre pigment, magically attractive; but it is also the colour of blood, including menstrual blood, which has ambivalent associations. Red, however, seems to be given more overt significance as an ambivalent category than white is. This difference would seem to lie in the fact that white is dominantly associated with men, while red is more closely linked to women. The more explicit ambivalence of red could thus be seen as a result of the fact that women themselves occupy a more ambivalent status in society, precisely because they have dual affiliations, to their natal as well as to their marital clans.[14]

Black, as we have seen, is clearly associated with males, and black charcoal with male aggressiveness in particular. The ambiguity of black thus does not result from its association with different substances (as in the case of red, from ochre and from blood) or from different aspects of substances (white lime as a 'bright' pigment or as a dry, powdery dust), but from an evaluation of aggressiveness itself: we have argued that although it is valued by men, it is also complemented by, or counterposed to another value, that of inter-group friendship. Hence charcoal is both good (for decorating) and bad (it is characteristic of warfare), and the colour which stands for it becomes similarly ambivalent. We should distinguish, then, between *referential ambiguity*, as in the case of white and red, and *evaluative ambiguity*, as in the case of black.

We can also suggest that the aggressive import of black is played down in the context of festivals. We have seen that dark plumes, faces, wigs, etc. are appropriate to men in two contexts: warfare, and festivals in which antagonism between groups is marked. In both cases the darkness overtly signifies that the wearers' ancestral spirits have come to help them, and in warfare it further signifies hostility towards the enemy. As we have argued earlier, this meaning is covertly carried over into the context of exchange festivals, although it appears there in a muted form: informants say that at festivals dark decorations disguise men and make them impressive; they do not directly say that such decorations are meant to intimidate the recipients or the spectators. This suppression of the aggressive import of black occurs because of the dogma that festivals are quite different from warfare; but as we have seen, the dogma is undercut by clear similarities between the two, and thus, we suggest, the suppression of 'transfer' between the two contexts is only a weak one.

Again, in warfare, decorations were worn only when men were fighting against major enemies. We have noted earlier that when warriors wore bright ornaments for fighting, these were said to have the *same* function as dark decorations: to frighten the enemy. This seems to be another case of suppression of associations. In warfare the connotations of attractiveness which bright decorations carry in festivals are quite inappropriate. Instead, we find that red, white, and other bright colours are given an aggressive meaning similar to that which red may have in spells and mythology.

We also noted in chapter four that against minor enemies no decorations were worn. We suggest here that there are two conditions which produce this situation. First, there is less aggressiveness against minor enemies, hence charcoaling the face and body is not necessary. Second, bright decorations are actually put on and receive emphasis at exchanges between such minor enemies, and to wear them also in warfare might lead to an intrusion of associations. The net result is that no decorations are worn at all. Such an intrusion would be much less likely in the context of major warfare, for between major enemies there were traditionally very few friendly links, and no war payments or *moka* exchanges passed between them.

In conclusion, we compare the use of colours in mourning with their use and meaning in decoration. It has been one of our themes that self-decoration enhances the person; mourning involves a reversal of this, for the mourner is expected to harm and even mutilate his own body. Hence many of the actions of persons in mourning can be seen to reverse acts of decoration.

At funerals both men and women tear at their hair and smear their bodies with clay, mud, or ashes. Men remove their wigs. The mourning is much more elaborate if a big-man, who pre-eminently represents the strength (or 'grease') of the group, has died. The act of tearing out one's hair is noteworthy here. It is precisely the reverse of emphasising one's hair by constructing a wig for wearing at festivals (cf. Pl. 17).

The close female kin of the dead man, and his widow, as well as close male relatives, all smother ashes over their hair and bodies. As an alternative they may smear on white clay (*kaem*) and also various-coloured clays from yellow to orange (Col. pl. 31).[15] They plaster clay so thickly on the hair that it can no longer be seen. More distant kin can perform all these actions, too, and are likely to do so if it is a really important big-man whom they are mourning. In this context no one speaks of the clays as giving a bright or shining appearance to the skin. Instead informants speak of the ashes, and the muds that are plastered on wet and then left to cake on the body, as drying up the skin and making it feel 'bad'. Moreover, these substances are smeared all over the body, rather than carefully applied to limited areas as clays used in face-painting are.

Later, after a first set of pigs is killed as a sacrifice following the funeral, close female mourners don large netbags dyed black which they have been making while the initial period is in force, and at this stage they also traditionally cover their faces in soot (*nggoa*), not charcoal, specially prepared from a tree resin and mixed with grease to help it stick.[16] Men do not use soot in this way. The reason for the custom here is that the ghost (*min*) of the dead husband comes and stays in the netbags of his wife and close female kin, and the black colour of their faces is a sign of this. It is particularly the widow's duty to blacken herself in this way. The usage thus parallels the wearing of charcoal in warfare by men, but it is not said to indicate any aggressiveness on the part of the women. It is notable that here, outside the context of decorations (*moke*), women put the colour black on their faces, whereas men do not.

Mourning behaviour in fact reveals a number of contrasts with the act of decorating oneself. Decoration emphasises well-kempt, ample hair (=strength, life, well-being) while in mourning the hair is torn and plastered with mud (=weakness, death, grief). In decoration, paints are applied in powdered form to the face with care and for beautification; in mourning, wet clays are smeared carelessly as a disfigurement all over the body. Finally, decoration emphasises glossy, greasy skin, while mourners rather make their skin dry

167

and cake it with ashes. In this last example we find that ashes and white clay, which in other contexts stand for grease and health, stand in the context of mourning for their antithesis, dryness and death.

In considering the colours red, white, and black we have found that all of them within their range of reference include attributes that are incompatible with each other; so that each taken as a category could be said to be ambiguous. In the context of decorations, however, the potential ambivalence is not always relevant. Red, we would suggest, does have ambivalent qualities in decoration, through an intrusion of meaning from other contexts. The ambivalence of black we have posited is of another kind, stemming here from its use in two contrasting contexts of decoration (warfare and festivals), and we have noted that the ambiguity lies not so much in its meaning as in the evaluation which black decorations receive. The same is true of 'bright' decorations (red, white, and other bright colours included), whose meanings vary between these two contexts. In the case of white alone, however, its connotations in decoration seem relatively unambiguous. Although semen, like blood, has polluting as well as health-giving qualities, and although the same white clay that is put on in mourning is also used in face-paint, there seems to be little intrusion from these concepts and situations into the connotations of its use in decoration.

Interpretation of the colours used in decorations and in other contexts is thus a complicated matter. The same colour or the same binary colour opposition (such as red/black) may carry different loads of meaning in different contexts. It is not possible for us to say, as Turner[17] does for the Ndembu, that two of the colours in the triad of white, red, and black are unambiguously evaluated and only red is ambivalent, for, as we have been arguing, all three colours as such have ambiguous associations or evaluations. Usually, their meaning is unambiguous in a given context, but we have also argued that there can be transfer or intrusion of meanings from one context to another.

Two major contexts which are clearly separated, however, are those of decoration itself and of mourning; and in the context of decoration we have suggested that dominant meanings can be identified for the three colours, two of which are linked together as bright in contrast with the third which is dark. White stands for health, fertility, and attractiveness, and through the equation between health, grease and semen it comes to be most clearly associated with male fertility and clan continuity. Red, which like white is regarded as bright, also stands for fertility and especially for powers of attraction, but, through its latent equation with blood, it is most closely linked with women and thereby gains a tinge of ambivalence which parallels the ambivalent nature of affinal ties between groups. Black stands unambiguously for male strength and aggressiveness, and in that sense is opposed to red.[18] It represents the internal solidarity and external competitiveness of groups, which are counter-balanced by individual links of friendship between them.

We can now complete a suggested transformation of the colour patterns listed in Table 6 into their latent meanings (Table 7).

TABLE 7: *Summary of the latent meaning of decorations*

		Men	Women
CULTS	Female Spirit	Male fertility (with muted emphasis on female)	Lack of emphasis on female fertility, because this is polluting
	Wøp Spirit	Male solidarity and fertility	Female fertility
EXCHANGE	Large gifts between opposed groups	Male aggressiveness (opposition to other groups) plus clan fertility and friendship with other groups	Female contribution to male activities (i.e. 'productiveness')
	Smaller-scale, where less opposition	Clan fertility and friendship with other groups	Either these are shell gifts which are men's affair; or, if involving pigs, not enough to justify display of female productiveness
	Pig-killing festivals	Clan fertility; friendship with other groups; sexual attractiveness	Women attracted by men
	Pig-moka (with pig's tail aprons)	Clan fertility, with secondary emphasis on friendship with other groups	?Emphasis is on male 'grease', which is antithetical to female menstrual blood: like the Female Spirit cult. Secondary emphasis on female productiveness
WARFARE	Major warfare	Male aggressiveness (opposition to other groups); male ability to make others afraid	Women not involved (except as objects fought over)
	Minor warfare	Less male aggressiveness + suppression of friendliness = no decorations	Women not involved (except as objects fought over)

We have constructed this scheme of symbolic meanings for colours both from informants' statements and from what we know about the festivals, cults, and battles at which the decorations were actually worn. In analysing the results we have been led to develop the concepts of contextual intrusion, suppression, and reversal, which find no exact replica in what Hageners themselves say. All anthropologists are faced with similar difficulties in analysing their material, especially when they are dealing with topics such as mythology, art, or ritual. Bohannan[19] has summarised the difficulty by distinguishing between a folk system – the set of ideas and statements which a people themselves hold and make about some aspects of their society – and an analytical system, which an observer constructs using concepts from his own culture and discipline.

In our account here we have tried to give what the 'folk' ideas themselves are, and then to relate the meanings of colours, given by the informants, to each other. In doing so, we have also translated these meanings into a more abstract form, and it is here that our operations have become in part conjectural. For example, while Hageners say that charcoal is favoured by men, disguises them, shows that their ancestors are helping them, and makes them look large and frightening, we have interpreted this as meaning that charcoal stands for 'clan strength and aggressiveness', and have suggested that men's dark decorations as a whole carry this same meaning, stressed in some contexts more than in others. We have then attempted to push this analysis further by explaining why certain meanings are stressed and combined with others on particular occasions. Ultimately our interest is in explaining the behaviour of Hageners; and in understanding what it means to a row of men to dance in a proud amalgam of dark and bright decorations before their allies, rivals, enemies, and spectators.

Self-decoration as art

At the beginning of the book we commented that Hageners do not make elaborate masks, figures, and the other kinds of objects which one associates with New Guinea art. We have seen that what does receive elaborate attention, involving aesthetic criteria, is decorating the person. The Hageners, rather than making figures or paintings to represent their ideals, transform themselves into an ideal state by self-decoration. Although the dark elements in their decoration are meant to disguise them, their aim is not impersonation of some other identity but aggrandisement of their own.

In this sense their art is not representational. The decorations do not submerge the actor and make him represent some other person, animal, or spirit, as masks and costumes do in many other cultures. The individual is transformed only in so far as he is invested with certain ideal qualities or marked out as holding a particular role for an occasion.

Thus, one message of decorations is simply that an individual is a donor at an exchange festival, a warrior ready to avenge past wrongs, a big-man, and so on.

Second, the decorations attribute to the actor an emotional state felt to be appropriate to a certain role. Donors decorate themselves lavishly because they are supposed to be triumphant in celebrating success; warriors cover themselves in dark charcoal to make themselves terrifying and to increase their aggressive confidence. In this case the individuals involved may or may not feel these emotions, but clearly they are ones which can be felt.

Third, decorations may demonstrate abstract and ideal qualities, which are also predominant social values. Thus dancers at a fertility cult conceive of them-selves as displaying the health and vitality which they claim performance of the cult has brought them. And at exchange festivals the bright attire of the dancers indicates their prosperity and is a sign that they are at harmony with the ancestors.

But self-decoration also conveys messages that the people themselves may not state in any explicit way. On occasions when people decorate there can be conflicting elements in the situation, and this may be expressed indirectly in the decorations. Thus at exchange festivals Hageners wear a mixture of bright and dark ornaments, and by elucidating separately the significance of 'brightness' and 'darkness' we are able to see that these two qualities correspond to two values which are both important in Hagen society: inter-clan friendship, and intra-clan solidarity and aggressiveness towards rival clans. As these two values are to some extent opposed, it is not surprising that informants do not call attention directly to them both when discussing decorations. Nevertheless, we argue, the message is there in the decorations themselves, and the clues required for reading it are found in other contexts when persons discuss the meaning of bright and dark items of decoration separately. The decorations for a particular kind of festival are thus not only combined to achieve effects which the Hageners specifically recognise, but may also indicate an amalgam of diverse values that does not otherwise find expression. Like any other art form, self-decoration carries its own symbolic load, and transmits messages that are not explicitly replicated in other media.

The opposition between dark and bright elements is linked to the opposition between men and women, which in Hagen, as in all New Guinea Highlands societies, is an important one. The values of strength and aggressiveness are predominantly associated with men, those of fertility and friendly relations with women. But, unlike the attribution of sex itself, these values are to some extent free-floating. Without making their decorations exactly like women's, men can incorporate into their costumes elements that stand for values which are in other contexts associated with females; and women can do the same in relation to males. Thus men can wear a profusion of red ochre to make themselves attractive in their *kilt* wig; the wig itself indicates that they are still male. And women can wear lavish head-dresses for *werl* dancing, which are said to over-shadow them and make them dark like men, but the style and profusion of the feathers, and the women's red face-paint, differentiate them from the men. The decorations make it possible for part-oppositions and equations between the sexes and between other categories of dancers to be made, so that the messages become intricate.

Decorations, then, make statements about social values. The two central values are clan solidarity and prestige, and individual wealth and well-being. This suggests why it is so appropriate that Hageners decorate *themselves*, for it is men and women as persons who remain the points of reference of these values. This is not to deny that the value of group solidarity could be expressed in many other ways, for example by cult buildings or statues. But decorations and dancing provide an excellent mechanism for demonstrating both of the two values together. Moreover, the values are to some extent complementary rather than opposed. In exchange festivals, for instance, it is through the efforts of each individual to raise pigs, shells, and decoration items through his own in-laws, extra-clan kin, and friends that the whole clan is enabled to put on a successful display. Dances themselves provide an opportunity for demonstrating both clan solidarity and individual excellence. Hageners hold, in fact, that in this context the prestige of the clan coincides with that of its members. It is themselves that they decorate, for it is through men's personal achievements that renown is brought to them and their clan alike.

Hagen and other New Guinea societies: a comparative note

The Hageners' concentration on self-decoration seems to be typical of New Guinea Highlands societies. Other New Guinea societies, for example those of the Sepik River area, which seem just as segmentary, competitive, and marked by male/female dichotomies as those of the Highlands, and often show as great an emphasis on self-decoration at festival times as the Highlanders do, nevertheless also produce elaborate paintings and wood-carvings, important in their rituals. In the Highlands such elaborate paintings and carvings are absent.

In the Eastern Highlands, in areas near Kainantu,[1] men sometimes wear large emblems, painted on a backing of bark-cloth, at non-religious ceremonies, which are allowed to fall into disuse when the ceremonies are over. Similar emblems are associated with initiation ritual among the Gahuku-Gama.[2] There are also stylised boards, known as *gerua*, which signify ancestral power and are made for ritual connected with pig festivals in parts of the Eastern Highlands and near-by areas of the Western Highlands; for example among the Siane,[3] Gururumba,[4] Nondugl people,[5] and Kuma.[6] Beyond Hagen in the Western Highlands, some of the Enga have anthropomorphic cult figures.[7] And in the Southern Highlands the Wiru people make stylized wickerwork representations of male and female figures which they wear at cult festivals.[8] Ryan[9] describes how Mendi carve human images on the posts of their ceremonial houses erected during a sequence of exchange festivals: the figures represent dead warriors and are displayed to disgrace other clans that have not made compensation payments for their allies killed in war. Finally, we may note that masks[10] are sometimes made in the Highlands (occasionally in burlesque mood for festivals).[11] But these figures and masks cannot compare in elaborateness and ritual importance with those which the Sepik peoples construct. How is it, then, that the Highlanders have not developed art forms of this kind?

Such a question, of course, scarcely lends itself to a clear answer. However, it is possible to point to a feature of Sepik cultures which may be relevant here. One correlate of carvings and paintings in these cultures and elsewhere in Melanesia is the presence of graded initiatory societies. Older males hold authority in these, and ration out the acquisition of ritual knowledge to their juniors. The senior men may possess authority outside the cult society as well. Art objects in these cultures often *are* the cult secrets, which are revealed gradually in a number of stages to initiates; carvings and paintings may decorate the houses where initiations are held.[12]

There are many Highlands societies also[13] in which some form of male or of both male and female initiation is practised. In these, and in the Spirit cults which are a feature of Hagen and other Highlands religions,[14] there could have been elaborate representations of spirits in art form. Instead, as the central symbols of these cults, we find relatively simple objects: sacred flutes, stones, upright stakes, and springs of water. It is these which are used in ritual to express values of male strength, clan solidarity, fertility, and the like; while expression of the same values is repeated in the dances which follow cult ritual sequences through the actual decorations put on by the performers.

Two considerations may help to explain this lack of elaborate art in cult rituals themselves, at least in Hagen. (What we have to say applies to Hagen in the first place, and may be true of other Highlands societies as well.) Rituals have the purpose of increasing fertility, health, and prosperity, and the focus in cults is on actions designed to achieve these ends, not on the revelation of spirits in tangible form. Similarly, Hageners emphasise not the physical nature of ancestral ghosts but their unseen presence and influence over health and moral behaviour. In this sense, their conception of the spirit-world is abstract. Yet at the same time their chief cult objects often stand directly for parts of the human body which especially indicate strength and fertility. Thus in the *Wop* cult an upright stake is explicitly described as phallic, a spring of water is said to help men procreate children, and long cult stones referred to as 'male' are buried with 'female' mortars in a position which imitates the act of copulation. These cult objects also stand for the Spirit sacrificed to in the cult itself. Anthropomorphic representation of the spirits is thus replaced on the one hand by cult stakes and stones, etc. which are their central symbols, and on the other hand by statements linking these symbols to parts of the human body.

If we turn to self-decoration itself, there also we find a lack of representational art. The process of decoration in Hagen is not representational but metonymical:[15] that is, when Hageners wish to associate themselves with magically powerful things, such as birds, they do not construct masks, carvings, or paintings of these. Instead they actually take *parts* of the birds, their feathers, and attach these to themselves as decorations. Nor do they attempt to represent these birds or to impersonate them in their dances. Rather, they use the bright qualities of these feathers to enhance their own bodily attractiveness. Clearly, the operation of decorating here is quite different from situations in which men represent ancestors or other spirit-beings or animals. Hagen dances and rituals have their foundation in mythology, but Hageners are not explicitly concerned to re-enact the myths in their performances. Instead, they have a more ethological version of how they came to set up ceremonial grounds and display at them: they say that they follow the bower bird, which clears a space to dance in and attracts sexual partners to itself.

Two factors, then, which accompany elaborate carvings and paintings in the Sepik area and elsewhere in New Guinea – the presence of graded initiatory societies which reveal secrets to their cult followers, and the enactment of myths in dance-forms – are both unknown in Hagen, and the same is true of some other parts of the Highlands. To say this is merely to point to a pair of correlates in the situation; we do not claim that it explains the situation itself.

Items other than the body which receive some decoration

Objects, apart from weapons and drums, which receive some decoration and have not yet been discussed include: ceremonial netbags, cult stones, cult houses, men's houses, Jew's harps and flutes, armband sticks, and drinking gourds.

1. Ordinary coarse netbags used by women for carrying sweet potatoes and the like are made from a plain twisted fibre. Special ones, given to newly married brides to wear at festivals, for example, are dyed in stripes with purple plant-juices and have flecks of marsupial fur rolled into their thread also. The technique of their manufacture is the same as that used for making men's long ceremonial aprons (cf. Pl. 31).

2. Cult stones are painted in the bright colours which Hageners associate with attractiveness and fertility. Those for the Female Spirit cult are painted red all over. Some of the stones are prehistoric mortars, which have been dug up by chance in gardens. Present-day Highlanders usually say they have no idea how to manufacture stones of this type.[16] For cult celebrations the mortars are often striped or painted in divisions with red, white, and yellow. Strauss[17] reports that bright ochre colours are described in a myth as left behind by Sky Spirits (*Tei wamb*),[18] who are, in a remote way, controllers of human fertility; and this would fit with the argument of our book and with the use of these colours for painting cult stones.

3. For the Female Spirit cult the houses in the cult enclosure are festooned with layers of silver-grey *mara* and reddish-brown *kundumb*[19] leaves. In the *Wɵp* cult the high fence which shuts off the cult enclosure has a huge arch

of alternate rows of these leaves bent over it (Col. pl. 29). The same silver and brown foliage, along with red cordylines and green mountain moss, also decorate the sacrificial earth oven in this cult. Bright colours appear in the garb of the rituals experts: they bind red leaves to clubs which they use for killing pigs and arrange the same leaves in a fan above their fore-heads (Col. pl. 28). (Big-men carried similar clubs at a festival in the lower Nebilyer Valley in 1967 as a sign that soon they would be joining in a huge pig-killing.)

4. In Kaembia, a part of the Nebilyer Valley which has close connections with the Imbonggu area to the south, the verandahs of men's houses are decorated. Bamboo strips make vee patterns across wall boards, and continuous series of chevrons are scratched on the boards themselves; bunches of decorative dried leaves hang from the open gable-ends. (This last feature also appears all over the Melpa- and Temboka-speaking areas, and is probably not peculiar to them either. In particular, houses built to display shell valuables are adorned in this way, the leaves being those which have the magical power to attract wealth.) In Kulir, in the western Nebilyer, men's houses close to the cult places may have woven covers over the front skirting-board of their verandah end. Unimportant men should not sit on this board, and are sarcastically invited to do so by big-men, implying 'Who do you think you are? A leader?'

5. Jew's harps and flutes are made of bamboo; only a special kind of narrow-stemmed bamboo is suitable for the latter. Their surfaces are criss-crossed with burnt-in or nowadays razor-cut designs: rectangles, chevrons, diamonds, or triangles.[20]

6. Armband sticks are decorated like the Jew's harps and flutes, and are also made of bamboo. Each design has a name, likening it (for example) to an insect's wings (*lklaemb ndi*) or to the sloping surface of thighs (*poklaemb kil*). These two terms employ exactly the same logic as do some of the names for designs produced in face-painting. Moreover, *lklaemb ndi* is recognised as the same as the *uklimb* ('navel') motif painted on shields; and another pattern cut on armband sticks, *mon kerua*, shares the name for an equivalent design painted on cheeks.[21]

   Men wear these sticks projecting from their wigs in a position similar to that for cassowary bone spatulae (and they also use similarly decorated pins to scratch at their hair through the wig). Women insert them in their armbands. They may pass between the sexes as signs of romantic favour.

7. Gourds, used as drinking vessels, have patterns which resemble the 'Greek-key' motif. The designs are either burnt in or scratched on with the thumbnail while the gourd's outer skin is still green.

   We may note that, with the exception of the drinking gourds, a household utensil, these objects either themselves contribute to self-decoration (netbags, armband sticks) or are items decorated in connection with festivals (cult stones, cult and men's houses). Although the musical instruments are not directly employed in festivals,[22] they are frequently carried around on the person, to be played during times of leisure.

Individual variation in head-dresses: the Ndika moka, 1967

We tabulate first the main contrasts between donors and helpers at this *moka*, and second, patterns of individual variation. We omit two boys who wore brown cassowary plumes and had brighter face-paint than their seniors. The latter feature equates them with women and girls, in contrast with men.[23]

1. Main patterns of feathers worn

	Donors	*Helpers*
Main feathers common to both groups	A. Red bird of paradise	
Main feathers which discriminated between the two	B. *Køi wal*	E. Eagle circlets
	C. Saxony sprays	F. *Kumin* circlets
	D. Sticks of Blue bird plumes	
Accessory feathers common to both groups	G. Cockatoo feathers round wig	
	H. White eagle feathers at base of main head-dress	

2. Combinations of feathers worn by individuals (excluding accessory feathers)

	Wig type		Feathers			Numbers of men
I. DONORS	Enga wig	+	A+B+C+D			6
	Enga wig		A+B+C			2
	Enga wig		A+B	+D		3
	Enga wig		A	+C		1
	Enga wig		A	+D		1
	Enga wig		A	+C+D		1
	Knitted head-net	+	A+B+C+D			2
	Knitted head-net		A	+D		1
	Knitted head-net		A			2
						—
						19
						—
2. HELPERS	Knitted head-net	+	A		+E	5
	Knitted head-net		A		+ F	5
	Knitted head-net		A		E+F	1
						—
						11
						—
			combined total			30
						—

REFERENCES AND NOTES

PREFACE

1. This in effect is true of all Hagen decorations. Forge has suggested for the Abelam a distinc⸍ *pages 1–19* tion between 'cult art' and 'decorative art', although decorative art derives its meaning from cult motifs (1967: 67). For Hagen we would comment that both cult decorations and those worn for a range of other occasions equally reflect the same basic social values (of wealth, social prestige, group continuity and solidarity and so on).
2. Adam (1954 ed.): 134.
3. Apart from their wealth objects (shells) the Hageners, and other peoples of Highland New Guinea, have a fairly scanty material culture. This might fit with the supposition that only in the last few centuries, since the introduction of sweet potato, have they switched from an economy based largely on hunting and gathering to one of sedentary agriculture (Watson 1965). Watson's ideas, however, have been criticised (cf. Brookfield and White 1968), and it seems likely that dependence on agriculture in the Highlands long antedates the possible introduction of sweet potato there.

CHAPTER ONE *The setting*

1. Cf. Leahy and Crain 1937; Champion 1932; Hides 1936; Vicedom and Tischner 1943–8, vol. 1.
2. Cf. Wurm 1961; 1964. Also Bowers 1965; Cook 1966. Kauil may also be rendered Køwul, Kaugel, Kakoli, etc.
3. Cf. Franklin 1965; Leahy and Crain 1937: 222.
4. Language boundaries are also by no means a simple matter. Cf. Wurm and Laycock 1961. For a survey of Highlands cultures see Read 1954.
5. Cf. Salisbury 1962.
6. E.g. Brookfield and Brown 1963; Rappaport 1968.
7. Strathern, A. J. 1966a.

CHAPTER TWO *Decorations and how they are obtained*

1. Strathern, A. J. 1966b: 135ff.

2. Salt came from springs in Enga country to the west of Hagen (Meggitt 1958). Axes were *pages* 19–31 made in the Jimi Valley and at Abiamp in the Wahgi Valley (cf. Strathern, A. M. 1965 with references). Ceremonial axes were originally used in bridewealth, and the version of them made for the tourist market today is still carried in dances. Their elegant balancers and fine green or black blades excited the admiration of the early explorers (e.g. Vicedom and Tischner 1943–8, vol. 1, 120, and Leahy and Crain 1937).

3. These payments were to ensure healthy growth in children. If not made, it was thought that maternal ghosts would make the children sick.

4. Zoological terms for some of these shell types are: pearl shell – *Pinctada margaritifera* Lightfoot; bailer – *Melo amphora* L.; cowries – *Cypraea moneta*; nassa – *Marginella* sp.; green snail – *Turbo marmoratus* L. We thank Dr A. Bidder, Curator of the Museum of Zoology, Cambridge, for help with these identifications.

5. The bailer is a large shell – its smooth white surface may cover the whole chest – and is perhaps more impressive as a single item than the cowrie or nassa. Wearing bailers is specifically stipulated as desirable in some contexts, e.g. for the Female Spirit cult (see chapter four).

6. In the past only a thin rim of resin was placed round the shell (cf. Vicedom and Tischner 1943–8, vol. 1, Pl. 4, No. 1; vol. 2, Pl. 2, No. 2). This is a style now associated with the Kauil area. Vicedom and Tischner 1943–8, vol. 1, 118 illustrates the pearl shell handle.

7. The Hageners call by the term *parka* both the *raggiana* and the *salvadorii* subspecies of the Raggiana bird of paradise species, but distinguish the latter as *parka ndip*, 'parka fire', from its scarlet flanks. What we refer to as the White bird is *Paradisaea minor*, called *kuri* by the Hageners (Rand and Gilliard 1967: 495–7). We shall use abbreviations of this kind (Red bird, White bird) for certain species where the context makes it clear which they are. To demarcate this usage we employ capitals. Thus 'red bird' is a red bird, but 'Red bird' is the *parka*.

8. Cf. Bergman 1957: 122, Attenborough 1960: 97, Wallace 1898, and Gilliard 1953, 1955 for native methods of catching birds of paradise; Bulmer 1968a for hunting techniques in general.

9. The silver leaves are called *mara* (Lauraceae); the rusty-brown *kundumb* (Melastomataceae *Astronia* sp.); the fern is *nøng* (Cyatheaceae *Cyathea* sp.).

10. Cf. Strathern, A. J. and A. M. 1968.

11. In 1968 stone axes were included in an unusually large, archaic, and grand death payment for an important big-man.

12. Cf. illustrations in Vicedom and Tischner 1943–8, vol. 1, 120 ff.

13. Cf. Williams 1940: 134.

14. Vicedom and Tischner 1943–8, vol. 1, 119.

15. Distant visitors from Kauil or Ialibu may be invited by men planning a festival to make wigs for the dancers in styles typical of their own areas.

16. Some details of further artefacts which receive decoration, but which we have so far not specifically mentioned, are given in Appendix II.

17. The cooking was held by the Minembi Yelipi clan (Northern Melpa) before they danced to celebrate a *moka* in pigs and shells. In 1964 there were fifty-six men in this clan, of whom thirty-four were donors in the *moka* (*c.* 60 per cent).

18. The Female Spirit cult (see later chapters) performed by men of the Ukini Oyambo clan (Northern Melpa) late in 1964.

pages 36–54

1. Cf. Strauss 1962: 319.

2. Each stick records that eight or ten pearl shells have been exchanged as a set in return for two shells and a pig. Sometimes a son or a daughter may wear the father's sticks; or a woman her husband's.

3. Women may be said to own these pearl shell crescents in their own name, as they do their aprons, netbags, beads, and fur pendants. More valuable ornaments (mounted pearl shells, cowrie or nassa shells in the past, plumes) are owned by men. A woman may wear, on occasion, decorations belonging to her husband, and thereby display his wealth; or she may borrow decorations for a dance from male kinsmen.

4. In Melanesian pidgin, this sequence is known as *tanim-hed*.

5. Cf. Strathern, A. J. and A. M. 1968: 180. We discuss the *kilt* tree again later, in connection with the manufacture of special kinds of wigs.

6. Vicedom, the German missionary-anthropologist who worked in Hagen between 1934 and 1939, reports (1943–8, vol. 1, 101) that at this time the Hageners did not practise tattooing, although it was mentioned in one of the folk-tales which he collected. It is hard to tell whether tattooing has been introduced to Hagen through copying other peoples, such as Chimbu or Papuans, or whether it has been simply revived. The copying, if it is such, is not exact: Hagen facial tattooing is much slighter and more restricted than that of Chimbu, for example. Young men as well as girls may be lightly tattooed.

7. For a fuller account of bridewealth see Strathern, A. J. and A. M., 1969.

8. If the grease trickles straight down her nose, this is a good omen. It is the ancestors who send the omen.

9. These are Administration-introduced tasks. Most of the work on side roads is still done by hand. The logs support plank bridges.

10. These are elections of Local Government Councillors or of Members of the Papua and New Guinea House of Assembly.

11. Native Local Government Councils were established by the Administration in the early 1960s.

12. There are two main markets in the area, neither of them traditional: the Hagen town market and one set up by Dei Council (Northern Melpa).

13. A jealous husband may tear off his wife's decorations; to show her that she should not philander as if she were a young girl.

14. In the past bailer, nassa, and green-snail as well. A fuller account of *moka* is given in Strathern, A. J. 1966b and forthcoming.

15. Called *nde mbo kanan*, 'ceremonial tree dance', by Vicedom (1943–8, vol. 1, 245–6), from the fact that the dancers encircle the ceremonial tree planted at the head of the dancing ground. See also Strauss 1962: 115.

16. Vicedom (1943–8, vol. 1, 246) makes this point.

17. Contrast Kuma (Wahgi Valley) practice (Reay 1959: 156).

18. Cf. Reay 1959: 118 for a similar oratorical style in Kuma.

19. This is Northern Melpa usage. The Central Melpa call both the men's and the women's circular dances *mørli*. It is this dance which Leahy and Crain illustrate (1937: opp. p. 193).

20. Melpa *amb mui pukl wal*. There are two variations of this. In one (*amb mui pukl wal* proper) the emphasis is on the earth which the woman smothers over her head and the scraps of food (rind, peelings, leaves) she has in her netbag. The import is a reminder to enemies or rivals of their taunts that the group's land is bad, its produce poor, and the food they eat is

offal (i.e. they have no wealth). In the other (*wur wur*) the woman may carry more direct *pages 54–62* symbols of wealth: the pig⁄tusks and nuts, along with leaves associated with magic for drawing in valuables. The group's enemies have accused them of being weak like women, so it is their women that the men decorate, implying that they have riches enough, which they will display in good time. These messages may be directed at traditional major enemies, or else at allies, impatient for the expected exchanges, who have accused the clan of having no resources.

21. Female Spirit is a literal rendering of the Melpa *Amb Kor*; the *Wøp* Spirit is thought of as male. The Northern Melpa do not perform the *Wøp*, or have not so far performed it. In the circulation of cults between clans, the performing clan pays ritual experts for knowledge of the cult spells and actions. In the lower Nebilyer Valley, a variety of other cults is practised (e.g. *Palyim, Kopiaka, Engawakl*), but we cannot discuss these here. An important pair⁄cult of the *Wøp*, the *Eimb*, seems not to be planned currently by any group. Mission activity may cut short the progress of these cults through all the Hagen groups. Fairly detailed accounts of the two we discuss here are given in Vicedom and Tischner 1943–8, vol. 2, 423 ff., and Strauss 1962: 425 ff. Our account is based on our own observations also. We give only enough detail to establish the rough meaning of the cults and the sequence of events in them.

22. Cf. Bulmer, R. and S., 1964.

23. At one performance in 1964 they did both. The mission had weakened taboos in this area.

24. By the Epᵉkla⁄Eilya pair of tribes, in the Kulir part of the Nebilyer Valley, west of the Nebilyer river.

CHAPTER FOUR *Decoration sets*

1. One such exception would seem to be the designation given to women who dance to indicate that their husbands will be making *moka* in the distant future (*peng pokla werl* or *peng pokla moke*, see below and note 20), where the phrase describes the effect that the decorations have of covering the body but neglecting the head. In the case of the major decoration sets worn by men, there are no terms to indicate the attire apart from those that refer to the type of dance being executed or the occasion of the display.

   Feather assemblages receive a few metaphorical designations. Feathers pinned thickly together on a wig may be described as forming a 'nest'; tall feathers rising above a base of smaller ones may be called a 'nose', while the latter are a 'tail'. But most other terms refer simply to the way different plumes are skinned, stuffed, split up, and tied together. Apart from *køi wal*, a made⁄up ornament but which itself is always part of a bigger total assemblage of feathers worn, there are no specific terms for sets of feathers comprising a head⁄dress.

2. By this we mean that a person cannot jump from one set to another on his own initiative, nor can he introduce new combinations of items that would make up sets different from the accepted ones. As we indicate later, however, he may dance without a full set (whether he regards himself as able to participate or not depends on how many of the main items he has assembled). There are also recognised alternatives to a main set worn in some contexts (see this chapter, note 47).

3. Shells and furs are also important items of decoration (see chapter two) and may rank with feathers in the emphasis placed on obtaining them. In discriminating between different occasions, however, they are not diagnostic of sets to the extent that feathers along with wigs and aprons are. In this context we can regard shells and furs as accessories.

4. There are no Hagen terms which correspond precisely with the distinction we make here;

it is one we deduce from the emphasis given to different items in different contexts, and *pages 62–78* from our observations of how these items are used.

5. E.g. a kind of small *køi wal*, and the wearing of long cowrie ropes by adult men. (Vicedom and Tischner 1943–8, vol. 1, Pl. 8, No. 4; ibid., Pl. 3, No. 1.) The early accounts of Vicedom and Strauss for the Hagen area allow us to trace such changes in a way not possible for many of the other major Highlands areas.

6. This is also called *peng lepa*, from the *lepa* thread used in its manufacture. Both *køi wal* and *Enga peng* seem to have diffused into Hagen from the Kauil area, the latter most recently. Enga is the term for a congeries of peoples living west of Mount Hagen (cf. Meggitt 1965). Bjerre (1964: opp. p. 73) shows the *køi wal* worn along with a reddened head-net, but does not say exactly where the dancers come from.

7. These are congruences Hageners explicitly comment upon.

8. Crests of the Sulphur-crested cockatoo; or feathers of the immature Princess Stephanie's bird.

9. Cf. Vicedom and Tischner 1943–8, vol. 1, 114.

10. There seems, however, to be no particular 'meaning' in these patterns. Although the feathers are mounted in standardised designs, there is no particular significance attached to the designs as such. This is a feature the *køi wal* shares with face-painting (see chapter five). Sometimes Saxony feathers cross the plaque diagonally, dividing the whole field into four triangles.

11. Running water has various attributes; it is cool and fresh, bright and shining, and has qualities associated with life, as opposed to those of dry, dead things. Here the glistening Saxony plumes are deliberately placed to offset the dark *køi wal* (see chapter six).

12. It requires a forest environment between 4,400 feet and 6,300 feet above sea level, and its natural habitat is being cut into by advancing agriculture.

13. It is exuded by an insect.

14. Its feathers are grey-black or bluish, occasionally white-tipped (as in the case of the immature Palm cockatoo).

15. Thus the russet plumes of the Red bird, invariably worn above the *wal*, are specifically designated as 'bright'.

16. And in a sense he turned his rather poor assemblage into a seeming deliberate effect; he could quite easily have charcoaled his face all over, as everyone else did, but instead he drew attention to his relatively unusual appearance by partially streaking it. This is the only instance of such behaviour of which we were aware during our observation of festivals in Hagen.

17. Turkey and peacock feathers, from birds Europeans have introduced, are seen as substitutes nowadays for eagle and *kumin*. In this case they were probably obtained from the local Seventh Day Adventist mission and Hansenide centre.

18. Blue bird sticks can sometimes help to distinguish the donors, as in the Ndika *moka*. But in the Kawelka *moka* of 1964 they were sported by both donors and recipients. As we have seen, the politics of the occasion explain these variations. There are also micro-cultural differences involved such as the one we have already noted. Temboka men plant thick 'circlets' of eagle and *kumin* feathers in their wigs, while the Northern Melpa men line them on pieces of softwood, making it possible to arrange the Blue plumes to either side.

19. The lily is found growing wild in swamps, but the sedge may be planted. The former (*wenem*) makes a rather shorter skirt than the latter (*kukil*); both kinds were worn on this occasion. We may note that skirts made from these materials are everyday wear among

Enga peoples and to the south of Hagen, e.g. the Wiru; but in Hagen they are specifically reserved for festival attire.

20. This is a deliberate effect. The women are described as dancing *peng pokla werl*, their decorations are cut off (*pokla*) at their heads (*peng*): i.e. they do not dance with the feathers that would indicate their immediate involvement in *moka*. This is Central and Eastern Melpa usage; Northern Melpa do not seem to do this.

21. Cf. Vicedom and Tischner 1943–8, vol. 1, 138; ibid., Pl. 3, No. 2; Bjerre 1964: opp. p. 33. Strauss 1962: ch. 54.

22. The *poklambo* tree. The tree is consecrated to ancestral ghosts of the group owning the ceremonial ground.

23. The wearing of *kundil* has a further magical purpose: it is a 'strong' thing which endures and can be inherited, so its wearers will be as strong as it is. The *kundil* seems to have belonged especially to Temboka, where many *moka* customs apparently originated. We have never seen it worn. (We found precisely similar decorations, called *kangge*, among the Wiru people of the Southern Highlands in 1967–8. *Kangge* are also associated with achievement in the Wiru exchange system. Cf. Strathern, A. J. 1968.) Many of the customs surrounding *moka* which give us clues to our analysis have now disappeared under governmental and mission pressure. Mission-followers dislike pagan ritual; and the *moka*-makers are nowadays always in a hurry to finish their festivals before returning to Local Government Council tasks. *Moka* has been secularised and speeded up.

24. A term used because of their resemblance to European judges' wigs, in the effect they have of framing the face and reaching down to the shoulders.

25. Cf. Reay 1959: 160–1.

26. Cf. Gilliard 1955; Criper 1968: 273 ff.

27. Cf. Rappaport 1968.

28. We have seen examples, however, made by Central Melpa for display at the Hagen Agricultural Show. We heard by letter that a Central Melpa *ware* dance was performed with *koem* and *kuklnga* in 1968 (Kendika tribe).

29. Yamka tribe.

30. There was certainly no kind of rule against using women's hair for wig-making as there explicitly is among the Mae-Enga (Meggitt 1964: 223, note 13). Mae emphasise the weakening influence of women more than Hageners do.

31. The swiftlet is a bird of bad-omen, and in some contexts this attribute becomes relevant to the meaning of designs said to resemble swiftlet wings: see the later discussion on warfare decorations and shield designs. This was a connotation certainly not commented on in association with the *peng koem*. We suggest there is no further symbolism in this case beyond the metaphorical description of a pattern on grounds of resemblance – as we shall indicate is also true of many of the designations for patterns painted on the face (chapter five).

32. The paints used included red, yellow, and white. (One of the recently made wigs we saw (see note 28) also had vivid blue trade-store paint on it.) Here, the eagle breast feathers and *mara* leaves contributed white colouring, the cockatoo yellow, and the parrot red.

33. E.g. Elti and Yamka tribes.

34. One tribe (the R^{e}mndi) held a performance in 1964 with specific borrowings from Wahgi style: fragments of green-snail shell at the waist; a proliferation of Princess Stephanie tail feathers; circlets of parrot feathers; King of Saxony feathers curving up from the septum to the forehead; bands of beads round the head; multiple furs over back and chest; and shaved faces, stippled in bright colours. A performance in a previous year (by the Ndika Mila-

pages 89–96

kambo clan) included shaving the beard, wearing reddened head⁄nets, and arranging feathers to run down the cheeks – all in the Wahgi Valley style again.

35. The other Melpa groups allowed *peng kilt* to deteriorate after a dance was over. The *koem*, by contrast, is preserved carefully and inherited by sons. For further pictures of similar wigs from the Highlands cf. Simpson 1955: frontispiece, opp. p. 78, opp. p. 158.

36. Cf. Rappaport 1968: 202 ff.

37. We do not intend to suggest that these outfits are specific to these tribes, but to indicate that these were the groups involved in two occasions for which we have information.

38. There is in fact another tree whose resin may also be used; but in accounts of the manufacture of these head⁄dresses this is no more than a technological fact: it is not given the symbolic prominence of *kilt*.

39. The *kilt* tree, we may note, is in more general usage only one of a class of trees which Hageners see as sharing the same characteristics: they have red or purplish blossom and/or red berries, and they attract birds in flocks. All the head⁄dresses we have been discussing here may be compared in their brightness to the flowers and fruits of all these trees: the metaphorical link is not restricted to the *kilt* – the *kilt*, however, is one of the most prominent members of this category, and in the context of the *peng kilt* is given most stress.

40. The spell continues with a list of the groups whose girls will swarm to the dancer. An example of a courting spell which utilises similar imagery is given in Strathern, A. J. and A. M. 1968: 180. The *kilt* tree is specifically named in it (in duplicated form as *kiltikilt*). We may note at this juncture that spells (*møn*) are accorded an efficacy of their own; they are not addressed to ancestral ghosts as prayers (*kor atenga*) are.

41. Tambiah 1968: 189.

42. Boys not old enough to have wigs of their own, but who may dance at the end of a line of men, have similar temporary supports.

43. This they liken to their pleasure at following the swinging tails of a large pig herd, in the same way as lime put on their legs (see below) reminds the dancers of how they get splashed with the mud that brushes off from the flanks of their fat pigs. The *kng øi mbal* does not seem to have been worn in the past in Northern Melpa; it is typical of Central Melpa and Temboka. Similar aprons are worn elsewhere in the Highlands, for example by the Huli and the Wiru of the Southern Highlands. Strauss (1962: Col. pl. 1) shows Kauil men wearing it.

44. *Wønya pemb* (Northern Melpa) or *klamb* (Central Melpa).

45. In the past bright leaves were used to bespell the oil.

46. By a Kumndi group in 1967.

47. Pig's tail aprons are not very common, which is why not all the men wore them. Only those who had such aprons whitened their legs and wore *Miscanthus*. There were two further alternative sets of decorations, although dancers wearing the alternatives followed after the more prominent body of men in pig's tail aprons who were to the fore in the *kanan* formation. Some dancers wore the *wønya klamb* (whitened head⁄net) with the ordinary long ceremonial apron (*mbal omb*); others had head⁄nets reddened with ochre or else wore plain head⁄nets, with *mbal omb*. Their face⁄paint, leaf and feather decorations were similar to those of the dancers in pig's tail aprons.

48. One informant claimed it could be worn for all exchange festivals and for *mør* as well as *kanan* dancing. Strauss, in the photograph cited in note 43, shows Kauil men making shell⁄ *moka* who are wearing it, but we would not expect Kauil custom to be exactly the same as the Melpa. He also describes a performance of the *Eimb* cult at which leading men wore aprons

to which the tails of sacrificial pigs had been attached (1962: 424).

49. Gitlow (1947: 56) quotes Ross's account of a Female Spirit cult performance among the Central Mokei (Ross 1937: 132–3) at which the main dancers were followed by a number of men and boys smeared all over with charcoal and carrying weapons. Ross claims these were to guard the shells displayed in the dance. Perhaps these blackened 'guards' were specifically meant to *contrast* with the main dancers.

50. Cf. Vicedom and Tischner 1943–8, vol. 2, 421; Strauss 1962: 420. A 'feather tower' was worn by a big-man at a Kuli *moka* in 1968. (This was a further internal event in the Kuli series; the main dancers on this occasion had been among the helpers at the *moka* held in 1967. Their wives had also danced then (as category (b): see above).)

51. It is possible that the performance of 1965 by the Ep^ckla-Eilya was not entirely typical. Strauss (1962: 421) describes as standard for the very closely related *Eimb* cult a 'feather tower' decoration which only a few boys wore at the *Wøp* of 1965. Strauss also (p. 423) mentions elaborate face designs in white, black, yellow, red, and blue. Other accounts we have suggest that occasionally White and Red plumes were worn on top of a whitened head-net or a *koem/kuklnga* wig. (We also have references to *koem* and *kuklnga* being worn for the *Eimb* cult in the past.) In these it would seem that the fertility-brightness association was more stressed.

52. Cf. Rappaport 1968: 195, following Wynne-Edwards (1962).

53. Cf. Watson 1967: 64 for warfare decorations among the Tairora of the Eastern Highlands.

54. Sometimes made up of old feathers, these were not so flamboyant as the Red fans worn for *moka* and cults.

55. Actual shell ornaments could also be worn, as noted above, but men would tend to select smaller, inferior examples, in contrast with those they tried to obtain for festivals.

56. Compare the 'women with netbags full of greens' (chapter three) who blacken their faces.

57. Some further comments on mourning attire are made in chapter seven.

58. At least ten spear-types are recognised, but most are named after their materials, none from their decorations (chapter two).

59. Cf. Troughton 1957: 42–5.

60. Both *pokan* (Amaryllidaceae *Crinum macrantherum* Engl. (Stopp 1963: 20)) and *kuklumb* (Araceae) have associations with fertility and prosperity ritual, but we do not think these associations are in point here. As with many design names, it is a simple comparison of shapes which produces the terms: cf. note 31.

61. Rappaport (1968: 83) suggests that the custom of eating salted pig-meat before fighting had definite effects on the warriors' physical capacities.

62. A parallel to this has been described for the Mendi (Southern Highlands). Each stage in a sequence of exchange festivals has its distinctive set of decorations. There is a gradual build-up in the elaborateness of these till full ceremonial regalia are worn at the climax of a sequence. Visitors attending from other groups are decorated according to the stage their own festivals have reached (Ryan 1961: 211–18).

63. We know of apparently pathological cases, for example one in which a 'man' wears a woman's belt and tucks a woman's cloth in it to hide the man's apron he has underneath. He is bearded, but is said to have no organs diagnostic of either sex. People treat him with toleration, and he is regarded with some amusement.

64. E.g. Eliade 1964.

65. It is only under the influence of Europeans and coastal workers in Hagen that some men shave off their beards nowadays.

1. Few of the other colours, however, carry such direct associations. Apart from red ochre, the pigments used in face-painting have no intrinsic worth as valuables. Nevertheless, it may be said that people like to decorate themselves with earth pigments because the earth is a 'strong' thing, it supports people: it is on the land that they grow their gardens and build their houses.

2. The categories that follow are ours. The terms seem to fall into three main classes, and we group them together in order to give examples of each type.

3. We may have missed some points here through not pursuing the matter carefully enough; but we can say that there is certainly no overt emphasis on linking particular face designs with particular purposes in this way. Contrast, for example, Trobriand face-painting: the eyes are a seat of desire, and hence a focus of decorative attention (Tambiah 1968: 204). Hageners do not readily comment on such attributes of facial features. Perhaps this is because the emphasis in decoration tends to fall on the head as a whole, and the head as a symbol of strength and attractiveness takes over functions which might otherwise have been expressed by its parts.

4. *Kokea* (yellow) is the only other earth colour used for both decoration and mourning. *Kela* (red ochre) is emphatically not: nor is *wande* (orange) nor *muk* (blue). Further orange, brown, greenish, and yellow clays that may be smeared on wet in mourning all receive different designations. See chapter seven.

5. These terms in no way comprise formal categories: they are simply sets of descriptions that can be applied to indicate the effect of a person's face decorations. It is our impression that the painter himself does not aim to represent a specific object (e.g. pig's tusk): there is no personal 'meaning' that these designs have to the painter which is hidden from the observer (cf. Berndt 1959). (We may add that the use of metaphor here is quite different from its employment in spells.)

6. Chapter four; and cf. note 16 same chapter.

7. In contrast, for example, to Australian Walbiri totemic designs (Munn 1966). Munn has shown how some of these comprise composite named patterns which are built up of elements themselves named and carrying meaning of their own. The Walbiri designs she discusses are also representational; we suggest that this is not really the case in Hagen, where the names simply derive from a visual similarity between the patterns and other objects.

8. Category 3a can thus be known also as *waep nggørman*, though this is not so usual as *kaem nggørman*. Conversely, *nomong* occasionally may be specified as *kaem nomong*.

9. We note that the name for the pig's tusk motif echoes that for mythical cannibals who turn up in Hagen folklore (*nggu nggørman wamb*). This suggests an association between the design and the attribute of aggressiveness, but such a suggestion is conjecture on our part: no link of this kind was commented on by our informants; and in other contexts we have noted that links of this nature may be irrelevant to the 'meaning' of design names.

10. E.g. Vicedom and Tischner 1943–8: vol. 1, Pl. 11, Fig. 2; vol. 2, Pl. 11, Fig. 3.

11. It is interesting to note that younger boys receive a different treatment from older ones, who are becoming more like men. At the 1967 Ndika *moka* the face decorations of four youths who stood next to each other, at the end of the line of adults, showed an interesting gradation. The two youngest wore cassowary plumes only, and their faces were completely painted in yellow chevrons on a base of red (Pl. 72). Next to them was a slightly older lad, who wore *køi wal*. He, too, had chevrons on red, but they were more restrained in

style (Pl. 71). The youth beside him had the conventional charcoaled face of a man.

12. Men do not often have much exposed forehead to be so decorated. Their wigs and the furs round the brow have the effect of bringing the hair-line down, sometimes nearly to the eyebrows.

13. Strauss (1962: 423), however, gives an example where this was done.

14. Because of the magnificence of the display with its element of disguise. See further chapter six.

15. Face-paint can be given the overall attribute of being 'bright', as feathers can.

16. Husband and wife who might both be dancing as donors were thus in their face-painting sharply differentiated as persons of opposite sex.

17. Girls may wear a little charcoal for courting parties, which thickens the grease they smooth on their brow. A small amount of charcoal may also be mixed with the grease that men anoint their bodies with for dancing – not to blacken them (as in warfare) but to bring out the gloss on the skin.

18. However, Strauss 1962: Col. pl. 2 shows male dancers some of whom seem to have covered nearly the whole face in red; another photograph (Col. pl. 23) shows a man who seems to have a modified form of *nde ndokl waep* (as the Kuli women wore).

19. Cf. note 34, chapter four.

The Agricultural Show at Mount Hagen, attended by groups from all over the Western Highlands District, has spread information about customs and styles of areas beyond Hagen. See also chapter six. It is a striking fact that men of the Wahgi Valley from Banz eastwards seem to wear much brighter colours on their faces than Hagen men do (e.g. Simpson 1955: opp. p. 63, and opp. p. 78 where (apparently) men and girls are dancing together, differentiated by their aprons but wearing very similar wigs and plume-arrangements). Perhaps this emphasis on bright colours is connected with sexual attractiveness in the Wahgi cultures as well as in Hagen: it would then fit with the more overt emphasis on sexual themes in the Wahgi festivals.

CHAPTER SIX *Reactions to display*

1. This is one of the few instances which might be construed as an example of Hageners decorating themselves to *represent* something else – in this case a spirit. It is clear, however, that the decorations are not concerned to present a physical image of the Female Spirit, but emulate qualities which are attributed to her – brightness, etc.

2. A feature he related to Minj influence, although such circlets are also worn by Central Melpa.

3. In his own area men wear these as informal decorations but not for *moka*.

4. Southern Nebilyer men doing the *Wøp* cult dance wore such tails in 1965.

5. This awareness of change must have been sharpened since Europeans came, but it seems to be at least partly indigenous, and possibly helps to explain why the Hageners are able to cope with the notion of social change on the number of fronts which Europeans have introduced. Professor R. Bulmer has told us that the Karam have similar ideas, and consider that their culture was changing almost as much before the Europeans arrived in their area as it has done since (personal communication). (For our discussion on changes in decoration we are greatly helped by the photographs in Vicedom and Tischner (1943–8) and Strauss (1962).)

6. They used these as currency to pay for services, labour, produce, etc.

7. Vicedom and Tischner, vol. 1, Pl. 10, No. 3; vol. 2, Pl. 13, No. 2.

8. The styles are: hanging freely at the back; loosely fastened at the waist-band leaving the breasts free; pulled over the shoulders and knotted between or above the breasts; hanging

free but to one side so that it can be drawn over the body with a movement of the hand and arm. All these styles are named.

9. This is stressed more in the *Wǫp* than in the Female Spirit cult (cf. chapter three). This association of ghosts with *Wǫp* perhaps helps further explain some of the dark elements in this cult's decorations.

10. See Lawrence and Meggit 1965; introduction.

11. An expert is someone with knowledge of a particular spell (acquired through purchase or inheritance) which few other people share. Whereas most people know spells they can employ in gardening, few, for example, would know details of *moka* ritual spells. It is thus the possession of relatively unique knowledge which makes a man a spell expert. He is usually paid for his services, but his competence in this sphere does not itself lead to an overall high status or make him a big-man.

12. Decorations can be described as an omen (*temal*) of the ghosts, as can the appearance of certain animals and birds at particular times.

13. Cf. Forge 1967: 83. He comments that the Abelam artist is rewarded for the beauty he produces because this beauty is seen by others as power. In Hagen eyes, beauty among other things attracts wealth: exchange partners, seeing the men so handsome, must find them irresistible, a motif which also appears in the Trobriands (Malinowski 1922: 335–6; Tambiah 1968: 204) and in Dobu (Fortune 1963: 231).

14. Cf. Rappaport 1968: chapter five.

15. It may also be said that the enhanced appearance of the warrior makes his allies 'sorry' for him, so they rally in support.

16. *Kopong* (grease) includes in its referents pig-fat or decorating oil, semen, and flesh under the surface of the skin which makes people appear well filled-out. We have noted that grease applied in decoration is thought to make both men and girls sexually attractive. (A young man who hopes to draw girls into the line to dance with him may ask not his own wife but some other woman, perhaps a brother's wife, to anoint him; he is afraid of his own wife's jealousy, lest she mix magic with the oil to prevent him from looking handsome.) But grease also carries wider connotations of strength and attractiveness in general. Sexual attractiveness here is largely a matter of eliciting admiration: the aim is to be admired, not necessarily to make sexual conquests. Thus girls who praise a man and spend a night in his settlement (see above) are not supposed to have intercourse with him. In fact sexual intercourse itself is seen as draining away the very grease which makes a man not only sexually attractive, but also strong and beautiful in a wider sense.

17. When women danced *werl* their husbands prayed to their own (the husband's) ancestral ghosts – thus the *werl* women dance as wives, in the care of and committed to help their husbands. Nevertheless, it is also thought that a woman's own ancestral ghosts may accompany her dancing, which is why women in profuse decorations may be described as 'dark' and as 'like men' (see chapter seven). The presence of a married woman's ghosts does not, however, have the connotations implied when men speak of themselves as dancing along with their ancestors. In the latter case, the men are united as a clan group and the whole body of clan ghosts helps them. A woman's ghosts are not so important as a man's in this sphere, and we think that it is dominant elements of *male* decoration that are particularly associated with the presence of ancestors.

18. And in everyday attire men's heads are often wigged. Men say that women do not wear wigs because they have to carry netbags full of sweet potatoes on their heads (i.e. they do humdrum household tasks all the time). Men do not carry things on their heads.

Our material on the importance of head-hair to the Hageners provides another case to *pages 137–58*
place with those discussed by Leach in his essay on 'Magical hair' (Leach 1958).

19. For a general account of Hagen spells see Strathern, A. J. and A. M. 1968.
20. Given that natural objects are held to symbolise certain values, Hageners could have painted designs on their faces or worn masks or used decorations to *represent* these objects – and 'become' a bird of prey, and so on. (As, for example, in the Wantoat Valley: Schmitz 1963.) Their focus of interest, however, remains themselves, and they appropriate the desired values by simply attaching to themselves parts and bits of these objects. See Appendix I.
21. Strathern, A. J. and A. M. 1968: 180.
22. Strauss 1962: 220.
23. Cf. Forge 1966: 30.
24. From Stopp 1963: 19.
25. See chapter three, note 20.
26. Strauss 1962: 410; Vicedom and Tischner 1943–8, vol. 2, 421.
27. Stopp 1963: 18.
28. No explicit connection we have heard links this to the cassowary head-dress *køi kundil* (see chapter four).
29. Cf. Strauss 1962: 424.
30. *Keu* is the shine that white things in particular have; here the term for 'gleaming' would be a more general one such as *kont* or *eng nonom*; see Table 4, chapter seven, which sets out the Melpa terms involved in the designation of 'bright'.
31. Strathern, A. J. and A. M. 1968.
32. *Kuklnga*, *mara*, and *nøng*, for example, are forest plants; *kengena* can be found in both woodland and grassland bush.
33. Not all the trees planted in public places are used for decorations – for example, the casuarina is not. Casuarina trees are typically planted as fallow cover in old gardens.
34. Dried banana leaves, however, may be used as a bustle, because of their rustling quality.
35. Hageners do not regularly employ vegetable crops as valuables in their exchanges as some Highlanders do.
36. Each tribe is associated with a *mi* (usually some plant) and its members call on this substance when taking oaths before the ancestors. See Strathern, A. J. 1968: 549; Strauss 1962 *passim*.

CHAPTER SEVEN *The connotation of colour*

1. *Kumin*, Princess Stephanie, Sicklebill, and Superb bird cape plumes are dark too; but Hageners mention this quality especially of the *køi wal*, we think, because to them it is the appropriate wear for the donors at an important *moka*.
2. *Waep kerua* (see chapter five) especially may be singled out as 'the best'. Attitudes to relations between the sexes are discussed further in Strathern, A. M. 1968.
3. Turner 1966.
4. Turner himself notes that for the Ndembu this threefold colour classification yields to a twofold classification, through the fact that black is often a 'null member' of the triad. In Hagen symbolism, however, a positive use is made of the colour 'black' to represent male strength and aggressiveness; to the Ndembu it seems dominantly to represent 'death' (although it can also represent sorcery and sexual passion, both of which may perhaps be regarded as aggressive). Hence it is that black, or 'darkness', is not often a 'null member'

194

in a contrast with white+red, but is usually openly expressed.

Our discussion has some points of contact with Needham's work on symbolic classification, in which he describes triadic category systems within which the relationships are dyadic. Thus in a system consisting of ego's group, the groups to whom it gives wives and those from whom it receives wives, ego's group has dyadic relations with its bride-givers on the one hand and its bride-takers on the other. Cf. Needham 1962; also Levi-Strauss 1963: 132–63; Pouwer 1967.

The use of the terms 'contrast' and 'opposition' is worth commenting on here. By contrast we mean a juxtaposition showing striking differences; by opposition the relationship between a contrasted pair in which the members are of a contrary kind; in some cases this also implies antagonism. 'Contrast' is the more general term; it does not carry all the implications of 'opposition', which is why we use it to refer to the relationship between the categories 'brightness' and 'darkness'. It is clear enough that Hageners may think of these two as opposites, but not that they *always* think of them as 'antagonistic'.

5. Turner 1966: 49.
6. We are suggesting this at a conceptual level only; in practice men depend on friends and relatives for all their decorations, including the dark *køi wal*.
7. Contrast the Trobriands, where red has relatively unambiguous values; Trobrianders do not seem to attribute harmful, dangerous qualities to menstrual blood (Tambiah 1968: 204, quoting Malinowski 1929: 144–5).
8. Hagen ideas seem very close to those of the Mae-Enga here (Meggitt 1964, 1965). However, Meggitt does not say that semen can pollute milk, merely that semen and mother's milk are antithetical forms of vital fluid (1964: 209) and that a man should not look at his child for two or three months after its birth since its unclean skin would weaken him, and *also* his own male potency would destroy the child (1965: 165).
9. Turner 1968: 255 notes a use of red earth in Ndembu girls' puberty ritual which does not carry its usual connotation of menstrual blood, and he suggests that the general symbolism of the rite (which stresses white in this context) leads to a suppression of meaning.
10. There are in fact persons of notably lighter skin colour than others among the Hageners and neighbouring Highlands populations.
11. Hageners comment that the hands of a big-man are always greasy from the pig-meat he is constantly consuming.
12. A poor man does not spend much time in travelling and visiting: he stays at home, and sleeps by the hearth so that his skin is always dirty with ashes. This may also be said to be a characteristic of women as a class in comparison with men.
13. A woman who is afraid that menstruation will prevent her from dancing *werl* (see chapter six) may have this done for her over the festival period.
14. Whereas men are united as clan brothers, women, who link clans together in more tenuous relations of friendship through marriage, penetrate clan boundaries. For our style of argument here cf. Douglas 1966. Gluckman (1955: 98) made a similar point in explaining patterns of Zulu witchcraft accusations.
15. Men are likely to wear ashes on the first day of mourning only, whereas women, on whom more onerous duties fall, may keep themselves covered in ashes for several days. Close relatives of the deceased (of either sex) may also in their grief slap on black mud (*teringi*), scooped up from pl?ces that pigs have fouled.
16. This practice is no longer followed. Cf. Vicedom and Tischner 1943–8, vol. I, 99.
17. Turner 1966. Since writing this, our attention has been drawn to a similar analysis of

Karam colour categories: 'White, black and red, all seem to have both positive and negative associations' (Bulmer 1968b: 130).

18. Perhaps in other Highlands societies there is an *equation* between male displays of aggressiveness, dark colour, and sexual attractiveness. This may be so, for example, among the Tairora (Watson 1967: 73–4) and the Mae-Enga (Meggitt 1964: 215). Variations will depend, we would suggest, on patterns of relationships between affines, on the exchange system, on whether marriage is with enemy or ally groups, and on patterns of warfare and local group composition.

19. Bohannan 1957: 5.

APPENDIXES

1. Berndt 1959.
2. Read 1966: 139 and opp. p. 143.
3. Salisbury 1962: 32–5.
4. Newman 1965: 69.
5. Strathern, A. J., field notes 1968.
6. Reay 1959: 140.
7. Blank 1963: 907; Bjerre 1964. Wickerwork figures apparently used in fertility and increase rites are known from Ipili and in the Laiagam area (Mr and Mrs R. H. Gray, Mr. and Mrs. R. Lang, personal communications).
8. Strathern, A. J., field notes 1967.
9. Ryan 1961: 213–4.
10. Strauss (1962: 393) refers to a 'mask' made from banana stems which is put on by a man who 'represents' the Sky Spirits (see note 18) during an address to these spirits. Although Strauss says this was a cult commonly known round Mount Hagen, we have no detailed accounts of the mask worn at it nor of any parallel situation.
11. E.g. Gilliard 1953: 434; Berndt 1962: 299; Bjerre 1964: between pp. 48–9.
12. Cf. Forge 1967: 68. See also Schmitz 1963 for an account of a similar context for 'art objects' in north-east New Guinea.
13. E.g. Gahuku-Gama, Gururumba, Siane, Kamano, Kuma, Huli, Mae-Enga (bachelor associations). Cf. Allen 1967.
14. E.g. Mendi, Ryan 1961; and Kewa, Franklin 1965.
15. Cf. Tambiah 1968. They are certainly of 'functional significance' (Leach 1954).
16. Cf. Bulmer, R. and S., 1964; also Chappell 1964.
17. Strauss 1962: 424.
18. These Sky Spirits do not seem very important in Hagen affairs, and there is nowadays little ritual or cult activity associated with them. But see Vicedom and Tischner 1943–8, vol. 2, 416f; Strauss 1962: ch. 57.
19. *Kundumb* are specifically 'bright'. They range from brown to a pale yellow in colour. The latter may be described as *kewa*. They can also be worn along with the pig's tail apron. For their use on cult houses see e.g. Strauss 1962: 408f.
20. Vicedom and Tischner 1943–8, vol. 1, 242 illustrates a Jew's harp.
21. See chapter five.
22. Strauss (1962: ch. 58) suggests that sometime in the past flutes may have been used in cults, but Hagen rituals do not focus on flutes in the way that has been reported for the Eastern Highlands.
23. See chapter five, note 11.

BIBLIOGRAPHY

ADAM, L. *Primitive art*. Penguin Books, first published 1940, revised edition 1954.

ALLEN, M. R. *Male cults and secret initiations in Melanesia*. Melbourne University Press, 1967.

ATTENBOROUGH, D. F. *Quest in Paradise*. London, Lutterworth Press, 1960.

BERGMAN, S. *Through primitive New Guinea*. London, Robert Hale Ltd, 1957.

BERNDT, C. H. The ascription of meaning in a ceremonial context, in the Eastern Central Highlands of New Guinea. *In* J. D. Freeman and W. R. Geddes (eds), *Anthropology in the South Seas*. New Plymouth (New Zealand), Avery Press, 1959.

BERNDT, R. M. *Excess and restraint. Social control among a New Guinea mountain people*. University of Chicago Press, 1962.

BJERRE, J. *Savage New Guinea*. London, Michael Joseph, 1964.

BLANK, FR W. A fertility idol from the Western Highlands of New Guinea. *Anthropos*, vol. 58, p. 907, 1963.

BOHANNAN, P. *Justice and Judgement among the Tiv*. Oxford University Press, 1957.

BOWERS, N. Permanent bachelorhood in the Upper Kaugel Valley of Highland New Guinea. *Oceania*, vol. XXXVI, No. 1, pp. 27–37, 1965.

BROOKFIELD, H. C. and PAULA BROWN. *Struggle for land. Agriculture and group territories among the Chimbu of the New Guinea Highlands*. Melbourne, Oxford University Press, 1963.

BROOKFIELD, H. C. and J. P. WHITE. Revolution or evolution in the prehistory of the New Guinea Highlands: a seminar report. *Ethnology*, vol. VII, No. 1, pp. 43–52, 1968.

BULMER, R. N. H. The strategies of hunting in New Guinea. *Oceania*, vol. XXXVIII, pp. 302–18, 1968a.

BULMER, R. N. H. Karam colour categories. *Kivung*, vol. 1, No. 3, pp. 120–33, 1968b.

BULMER, R. N. H. and SUSAN BULMER. The prehistory of the Australian New Guinea Highlands. *American Anthropologist*, vol. 66, No. 4, pp. 39–76, 1964.

CAYLEY, N. W. *What bird is that? A guide to the birds of Australia*. Angus and Robertson, 1963 (third edition).

CHAMPION, I. F. *Across New Guinea from the Fly to the Sepik*. London, Constable, 1932.

CHAPPELL, J. M. A. Stone mortars in the New Guinea Highlands: a note on their manufacture and use. *Man*, vol. LXIV, No. 182, 1964.

COOK, E. A. Narak: language or dialect? *Journal of the Polynesian Society*, vol. 75, No. 4, pp. 437–44, 1966.

CRIPER, C. The politics of exchange: a study of ceremonial exchange among the Chimbu people. Unpublished Ph.D. dissertation, Australian National University, 1968.

DOUGLAS, MARY. *Purity and danger. An analysis of concepts of pollution and taboo*. London, Routledge and Kegan Paul, 1966.

ELIADE, M. *Shamanism: archaic techniques of ecstasy* (trans.). London, Routledge and Kegan Paul, 1964.

FORGE, A. Art and society in the Sepik. *Proceedings of the Royal Anthropological Institute* for 1965, pp. 23–31, 1966.

FORGE, A. The Abelam artist. *In* M. Freedman (ed.), *Social Organization: essays presented to Raymond Firth*, pp. 65–84. Frank Cass and Co. Ltd, 1967.

FORTUNE, R. F. *Sorcerers of Dobu*. London, Routledge and Kegan Paul, first published 1932, second edition 1963.

FRANKLIN, K. J. Kewa social organisation. *Ethnology*, vol. 4, pp. 408–20, 1965.

GILLIARD, E. T. New Guinea's rare birds and stone age men. *The National Geographic Magazine*, vol. CIII, No. 4, pp. 421–88, 1953.

GILLIARD, E. T. To the land of the headhunters. *The National Geographic Magazine*, vol. CVII, No. 4, pp. 437–86, 1955.

GITLOW, A. L. *Economics of the Mount Hagen tribes, New Guinea*. Monographs of the American Ethnological Society, No. 12, University of Washington Press, 1947.

GLUCKMAN, M. *Custom and conflict in Africa*. Oxford, Blackwell, 1955.

HIDES, J. G. *Papuan wonderland*. Blackie, London, 1936.

LAWRENCE, P. and M. J. MEGGITT. *Gods, ghosts, and men in Melanesia*. Melbourne, Oxford University Press, 1965.

LEACH, E. R. A Trobriand Medusa. *Man*, vol. LIV, pp. 103–5, 1954.

LEACH, E. R. Magical hair. *Journal of the Royal Anthropological Institute*, vol. 88, part 2, pp. 145–64, 1958.

LEAHY, M. J. and M. CRAIN. *The land that time forgot*. New York and London, Funk and Wagnalls, 1937.

LEVI-STRAUSS, C. *Structural Anthropology*. New York, Basic Books Inc., 1963 (original French edition, Paris, Plon, 1958).

MALINOWSKI, B. *Argonauts of the Western Pacific*. London, Routledge and Kegan Paul, 1922.

MALINOWSKI, B. *The sexual life of savages in northwestern Melanesia*. London, Routledge, 1929.

MEGGITT, M. J. Salt manufacture and trading in the Western Highlands. *Australian Museum Magazine*, vol. 12, pp. 309–13, 1958.

MEGGITT, M. J. Male-female relationships in the Highlands of Australian New Guinea. *American Anthropologist*, special publication on New Guinea, J. B. Watson (ed.), vol. 66, No. 4, pp. 204–24, 1964.

MEGGITT, M. J. *The lineage system of the Mae-Enga of New Guinea*. Edinburgh, Oliver and Boyd, 1965.

MUNN, N. D. Visual categories: an approach to the study of representational systems. *American Anthropologist*, vol. 68, No. 4, pp. 936–50, 1966.

NEEDHAM, R. *Structure and sentiment*. University of Chicago Press, 1962.

NEWMAN, P. L. *Knowing the Gururumba*. New York, Holt, Rinehart and Winston, 1965.

POUWER, J. Review of Van der Veen, The Merok Feast of the Sa'dan Toradja. *Journal of the Polynesian Society*, vol. 76, No. 1, pp. 104–8, 1967.

RAND, A. L. and E. T. GILLIARD. *Handbook of New Guinea birds*. London, Weidenfeld and Nicolson, 1967.

RAPPAPORT, R. A. *Pigs for the ancestors. Ritual in the ecology of a New Guinea people*. Yale University Press, 1968.

READ, K. E. Cultures of the Central Highlands, New Guinea. *Southwestern Journal of Anthropology*, vol. 10, pp. 1–38, 1954.

READ, K. E. *The High Valley*. London, George Allen and Unwin Ltd, 1966.

REAY, M. *The Kuma. Freedom and conformity in the New Guinea Highlands*. Melbourne University Press, 1959.

ROSS, FR W. A. Unga gets his share. *The Christian Family*, vol. 32, pp. 132–3, 1937.

RYAN, D. J. Gift exchange in the Mendi valley. Unpublished Ph.D. dissertation, University of Sydney, 1961.

SALISBURY, R. F. *From stone to steel. Economic consequences of a technological change in New Guinea*. Melbourne University Press, 1962.

SCHMITZ, C. A. *Wantoat. Art and religion of the Northeast New Guinea Papuans*. The Hague and Paris, Mouton & Co., 1963.

SIMPSON, C. *Adam in plumes*. Sydney, Angus and Robertson, 1955.

STOPP, K. Medicinal plants of the Mount Hagen people (Mbowamb) in New Guinea. *Economic Botany*, vol. 17, No. 1, pp. 16–22., 1963.

STRATHERN, A. J. Despots and directors in the New Guinea Highlands. *Man*, n.s., vol. 1, No. 3, pp. 356–67, 1966a.

STRATHERN, A. J. Ceremonial exchange in the Mount Hagen area. Unpublished Ph.D. dissertation, Cambridge University, 1966b.

STRATHERN, A. J. Sickness and frustration: variations in two New Guinea Highland societies. *Mankind*, vol. 6, pp. 545–51, 1968.

STRATHERN, A. J. *Moka. In* H. I. Hogbin (ed.), *Encyclopaedia of New Guinea*, forthcoming.

STRATHERN, A. J. and A. M. STRATHERN. Marsupials and magic: a study of spell symbolism among the Mbowamb. *In* E. R. Leach (ed.), *Dialectic in practical religion*, Cambridge Papers in Social Anthropology No. 5, Cambridge University Press, 1968.

STRATHERN, A. J. and A. M. STRATHERN. Marriage in Melpa. In *Pigs, pearlshells, and women*, M. J. Meggitt and R. M. Glasse (eds), Prentice-Hall, 1969.

STRATHERN, A. M. Axe types and quarries. A note on the classification of stone axe blades from the Hagen area, New Guinea. *Journal of the Polynesian Society*, vol. 74, pp. 184–92, 1965.

STRATHERN, A. M. Women's status in the Mount Hagen area. Unpublished Ph.D. dissertation, Cambridge University, 1968.

STRAUSS, H. (with H. TISCHNER). *Die Mi-Kultur der Hagenberg-Stämme im östlichen zentral-Neuguinea*. Hamburg, Cram, de Gruyter and Co., 1962.

TAMBIAH, S. J. The magical power of words. *Man*, n.s., vol. 3, No. 2, pp. 175–208, 1968.

TROUGHTON, E. *Furred animals of Australia*. Angus and Robertson, 1957 (sixth edition).

TURNER, V. W. Colour classification in Ndembu ritual. *In* M. Banton (ed.), *Anthropological Approaches to the study of religion*, Association of Social Anthropologists of the Commonwealth Monograph No. 3, pp. 47–84, 1966.

TURNER, V. W. *The drums of affliction*. Oxford, Clarendon Press and the International African Institute, 1968.

VICEDOM, G. F. and H. TISCHNER. *Die Mbowamb. Die Kultur der Hagenberg-Stämme im östlichen zentral-Neuguinea.* 3 vols., Hamburg, Cram, de Gruyter and Co., 1943–8.

WALLACE, A. R. *The Malay archipelago. The land of the orangutan and the bird of paradise.* London, Macmillan and Co., 1898 (first published 1869).

WATSON, J. B. From hunting to horticulture in the New Guinea Highlands. *Ethnology*, vol. 4, pp. 295–309, 1965.

WATSON, J. B. Tairora: the politics of despotism in a small society. *Anthropological Forum*, vol. 2, No. 1, pp. 53–104, 1967.

WILLIAMS, F. E. Natives of Lake Kutubu. *Oceania* Monographs No. 6, Australian National Research Council, 1940.

WURM, S. A. Languages of the Eastern, Western, and Southern Highlands, Territory of Papua and New Guinea. *In* A. Capell (ed.), *A linguistic survey of the south-western Pacific.* South Pacific Commission, Noumea, Technical paper 136, 1961.

WURM, S. A. Australian New Guinea Highlands languages and the distribution of their typological features. *American Anthropologist*, vol. 66, No. 4, pp. 77–97, 1964.

WURM, S. A. and D. C. LAYCOCK. The question of language and dialect in New Guinea. *Oceania*, vol. XXXII, No. 2, pp. 128–43, 1961.

WYNNE-EDWARDS, V. C. *Animal dispersion in relation to social behaviour.* Edinburgh and London, Oliver and Boyd, 1962.

ACKNOWLEDGEMENTS

Our acknowledgements and thanks are of two kinds: first to the institutions and organisations which have provided us with grants to carry out the field-work, during 1964–8, on which this book is based, especially to the International Federation of University Women and Cambridge University for enabling Marilyn Strathern to undertake work in Mount Hagen during 1967, and to Trinity College, Cambridge, which gave field-grants to Andrew Strathern during his tenure of a research fellowship there. Second, we wish to give our personal thanks to Professor Ralph Bulmer for help with bird identifications, and Miss Jocelyn Wheeler for identifications of plants (although neither is responsible for our errors in these fields); to Mr E. C. Evans for supplying us with the quotations from Shakespeare; and to all our informants in Mount Hagen, especially to Oke and Yakomb at Kelua, and to Ru at Buk among the Northern Melpa.

We wish to thank also the Australian National University for assistance with the production of the final manuscript, the map and figures, and the Pitt-Rivers Museum, Oxford, for permission to reproduce the shield on page 103.

Andrew and Marilyn Strathern
Canberra, May 1970

INDEX

Abelam people, 183 n. 1, 193 n. 13

Adam, L., ix

Aesthetic judgement, see Effects, Regional differences. Discussion of, 126–7, 130; of general appearance, 134, cf. 193 nn. 13, 16; of (*mør*) dance, 126; of face-paint, 99, 127; of feathers, 65, 119; of plants, 128, 147; of shells, 20; of wigs, 88; regional differences commented upon, 13, 128; significance of quality, 122; 11, 141, 153 ff

Agricultural show at Mount Hagen, see Hagen

Agriculture, 13, 14

Affines, loan ornaments, 11, 31–2, 78; 14

Allies, rivals, 44, 72, 134, 185 n. 20; supporters, 102, 193 n. 15; war payments to, 14, 48, 73

Amb Kør (Female Spirit), see under Spirit cults

Ambivalence, in evaluation of colours, 154, 158, 162 ff (summary, 168), 196 n. 17; to war ornaments, 34

Ancestors (ghosts), aid clansmen, 102, 104, 138, 164; dark decorations indicate, 101–2, 137; lodge in hair, 87, 94, 137; sacrifice to, 31, 43, 87, 104, 130, 132; success of decorations associated with, 22, 58, 112, 130 ff, 147; 40, 78, 148, 154, 184 n. 3, 185 n. 8, 188 n. 22, 193 nn. 9, 12, 17, 194 n. 36

Aprons, diagnostic items, 62, 66, 106; men's, 6, 10, 19, 22; *mbal omb*: dark, 65–6, 68; 96, 189 n. 47; pig's tail, 24, 89, 94–6, 189 nn. 43, 47, 48, 196 n. 19; women's, for dancing, 78, 187 n. 19; ordinary, 36, 37, 185 n. 3; worn with 'judge's wigs', 89, 91; 190 n. 63

Armband, 26, 89

Armband stick, 179

Art, and initiatory societies, 176: representational (c.v.) discussion, 171, 194 n. 20; in Highlands, 175–6

Ashes, see Mourning attire, 164–5, 167, 195 nn. 12, 15

'Attracting' wealth and opposite sex, aim of decorations, 16, 37, 40, 43, 54, 138 ff, 156, 158–9, 177; colour red, 26; grease, 138 (and c.v.); *kilt* head-dress 89–92, 189 nn. 39, 40; pig's tail apron, 96; plants, 144, 147; shells, 20, 140

Axe, see Stone axe

Banz, see Wahgi Valley

Bark belt, 24, 36

Bark-cloth, 28, 65, 87–8, 94

Beads (trade-store), 19, 37, 46, 129

Beards, and charcoaled face, 95, 116, 118, 137; 92, 124, 188 n. 34, 190 n. 65

Big-men, decide on decorations, 16, 62–3, 112; distinguished by decorations, 69, 83, 98, 105, 112, 179, 187 n. 16; mourning for, 167; own valuables, 20, 28, 30, 105; spokesman, 125, 132; 3, 6, 37, 40, 130, 154, 165, 193 n. 11, 195 n. 11

Birds, feathers worn for specific occasions, see Decoration sets, *Køi wal*; general, see Plumes.
Attracted to *kilt* tree, 90, 91, 92, 189 n. 39; *birds of paradise*: habitats, 21–2; hunting of, 22, 184 n. 8; Blue (*rudolphi*), 28–9, 65, 126, 187 n. 18; King of Saxony (*Pteridophora alberti*), see also *Køi wal*; worn by big-men, 69, 71; 28, 63, 65, 148, 158, 187 nn. 10, 11, 188 n. 34; Princess Stephanie (*Astrapia stephaniae*), festival called after, 75; 29, 103, 128, 140, 187 n. 8, 188 n. 34, 194 n. 1; Red (*raggiana*), symbolism, 141; warfare named after, 100; 21, 28, 31, 40, 65, 103, 128, 156, 163, 184 n. 7, 187 n. 15, 190 n. 51; Ribbon-tail (*Astrapia mayeri*), 29, 103; Sicklebill (*Epimachus*), 29, 65, 128, 140, 194, n. 1; Superb (*Lophorina superba*), 29, 128, 194 n. 1; white (*minor*), 21, 31, 32, 140, 184 n. 7, 190 n. 51; *other birds*: see Cassowary; bowerbird, 84, 177; eagle, symbolism, 141, cf. 84, 138; 28, 40, 187 nn. 17, 18; hawk, 40; lorikeet, 128, palm cockatoo (*Melpa kumin*), 28, 128, 187 nn. 14, 17, 18, 194 n. 1; parrot, 21, 29, 65, 128, 140, 188 n. 34; sulphur-crested cockatoo, 21, 29, 40, 187 n. 8; swiftlet, bird of ill-omen, 101, 103, 188 n. 31

Bjerre, J., 91

Black, see Charcoal, Colour symbolism

Blood, ambivalent attitude to, 162–3, 195 n. 7; ties between groups, 159, 160, 162; and red ochre, 162–3; 195 n. 9

Bohannan, P., 170

Bones, cassowary, 24; flying fox, 87; pig, 24

Borrowing decorations, apron, 10, 22, 24; *Køi wal*, 28; payment for, 11, 30–1, 78, 132; significance of, 26; sociology of, 28–32, 195 n. 6

Boys' decorations, see Decoration sets, also Youths'. Cordylines, 151; face-paint, 106, 117, 118, 191 n. 11; hair, 92, 189 n. 42; 37, 99

Bridewealth, occasion, 43–4; 20, 21, 28, 37, 39, 40

Bright, see Dark and light effects

205